THROUGH RUSSIAN CENTRAL ASIA

THE TOMB OF TIMOUR

THROUGH RUSSIAN CENTRAL ASIA

STEPHEN GRAHAM

With Photogravure and many Black-and-White Illustrations from Original Photographs

GYAN

Published by

Gyan Publishing House
5, Ansari Road
Daryaganj, New Delhi-110002
Phone: 011-47034999, 9811692060
E-mail: books@gyanbooks.com

Distribution Network
gyanbooks.com
India, USA, Canada, UK, Australia, France

ISBN : 978-81-212-4105-2 (PB)
First Published, London, 1916

2nd Impression 2020

Printed at: Gyan Press, Delhi.

Through Russian Central Asia
Author: Stephen Graham

Through Russian Central Asia

By

STEPHEN GRAHAM

With Photogravure and many Black-and-White Illustrations from Original Photographs

Cassell and Company, Ltd
London, New York, Toronto and Melbourne
1916

Contents

*

Contents

APPENDICES

List of Illustrations

List of Illustrations

Introduction

THE journey recorded in these pages was made in the summer before the great war, and although the record of my impressions and the story of my adventures were fully written in my road diary and in the articles I sent to *The Times*, I had thought to postpone issuing my book to some quieter moment beyond the war. But the days go on, and we are getting accustomed to live in a state of war; war has almost become a normal condition of existence. At first we could do nothing but consider the facts of the great quarrel of nations and the exploits of the armies. War for the moment seemed to be our life, our culture, and our religion. But things have changed. War started by concentrating us and making us narrow, but now it is giving us greater breadth. We have become more interested in the home life of our Allies, in the "after-the-war" prospects of Europe, in the future of our own British Empire and of the wide world generally. The war has given us a larger consciousness, and we have become, as some say, "Continental." In any case, we are much less insular. France and Russia have become real places to the man in the street, and the account he gives of them is more credible. Even our country labourer can say where Gallipoli is, Mesopotamia, Egypt, Salonica, Bulgaria, Serbia, though, indeed, I have frequently heard the latter spoken of as Siberia. "My son's gone to Siberia," says the countryman; "it's a cold place." Our imagination ranges farther afield, and young men of all classes think of making far travels when the war is over. We are not less interested in other things, but more; only less interested in the old suffocating business and industrial life of the time before the war, of the stuffy rooms, the circumscribed horizons, the dull grind. All eyes are opened wider, all hearts have greater hopes, and that which dares in us dares more. We are reading more, reading better, and, among other matters, are thinking more of foreign countries, empires, far-away climes. The war, bringing so many nations together, has touched imaginations. It has mixed our themes of conversations and enriched our life with new colours, new ideas. So, perhaps, the story of this journey and my impressions of an interesting but remote portion of the Tsar's Empire will not come amiss just now. Moreover, during the war many problems have become clearer, especially those of the British Empire, clearer, but none the less unsolved, and I feel that a study of a vast stretch of the Russian Empire, and of its problems and its prospective future, cannot but be helpful.

Among the letters sent me care of *The Times* there is one written about an article which has become a chapter in this book:

"Since I was a child and steeped myself in the 'Arabian Nights,' I have never been so enthrallêd as I was by an articlc of yours called 'Towards Turkestan,' which appeared in *The Times* long since, as it seems now (last May ?). I am an old, tired recluse. I have been reading for over sixty years. I'm very much extinct, but my desert also blossomed with your roses.

"Charm *inexpressible* breathed from the roses (I think they must have been the black-red sort). Strange figures —rich garments, all solemnised by, as it were, a twilight glamour made of magical influences. All so real, yet remote. I repeat, I have never been taken away so far since I was a child. There was another article which I cut out and lost . . . but I did not prize it as I did the Turkestan article, where figures both bizarre and dignified greeted you and bade you farewell with roses. And sunset steeps them in a golden haze. And they still move there whilst the traveller who has spell-bound them in his writing has gone on his way. . . ."

I have printed this letter because it was sweet to have it, and it touched me. May the roses bloom again!

I am indebted to the Editors of *The Times* and *Country Life* for permission to republish portions of this book previously printed in their columns, and to *Country Life* for permission to republish photographs.

Introduction

For these photographs, except those relating to the Altai, I am chiefly indebted to the professor of French at Tashkent Military School and to M. Drampof, of Pishpek. Special permission has to be obtained to enter Russian Central Asia, and, as I was going on foot, the possession of a camera might have led to the suspicion of military spying. So I had my camera sent to Semipalatinsk, which is in Siberia, and only used it on the Siberian part of my journey. My thanks are also due to Mr. Wilton, the courteous and able correspondent of *The Times* at Petrograd, who obtained for me my permit for travel in Russian Central Asia.

STEPHEN GRAHAM.

Through Russian Central Asia

I

LEAVING VLADIKAVKAZ

IN the early spring of 1914 I walked once more to the Kazbek mountain. It was really too early for tramping, too cold, but it was on this journey that I decided what my summer should be. Once you have become the companion of the road, it calls you and calls you again. Even in winter, when you have to walk briskly all day, and there is no sitting on any bank of earth or fallen tree to write a fragment or rest, and when there is no sleeping out, but only the prospect of freezing at some wretched coffee-house or inn, the road still lies outside the door of your house full of charm and mystery. You want to know where the roads lead to, and what may be on them beyond the faint horizon's line.

So it is March, and I am walking out from Vladikavkaz on the Georgian road, and only on a four days' journey—to the Kazbek mountain and back. Indeed, the road beyond is probably choked with snow, and there is no further progress. But I shall see how the year stands on the Caucasus.

The stillness of the morning—a circumambient silence. A consciousness of the silence in the deep of space. Three miles of level highway stretch straight and brown from the city on the steppes to the dark, blank wall of the mountains. Beyond the black wall and above it are the snow-mantled superior ranges, and above all, almost melting into the deep blue of the Caucasian sky, the glimmering, icy-wet slopes of the dome of the Kazbek. The sun presides over the day, and as a personal token burns the brow, even though the feet tread on patches of crisp snow on the yellow-green banks of the moor. No lizards basking in the sun, no insects on the wing, no flowers—not a speedwell, not a cowslip, not a snowdrop. Only little flocks of siskins rising unexpectedly from sun-bathed hollows like so many fat grasshoppers. Only an occasional crazy brown leaf that scampers over the withered fallen grass. There is vapour over the plumage-like woods on the hills, but no birds are singing. Nature can almost be described in negation, she shows so little of her glory; yet she makes the heart ache the more.

Persian stone-breakers, hammer in hand, sitting on mats by the side of the heaps of rocks; primitive carts lumbering with their loads of faggots or maize-straw or ice; horsemen like centaurs because of their great black capes joining their head and shoulders to little Caucasian horses—that is all the life at this season of the year of the one great highway over the mountains, the great military road from Vladikavkaz to Tiflis—no motor-cars, no trams, no light-rolling carriages with gentry in them, no trains.

Stopping at a sunny mound to have lunch, you

hear from a hundred yards away the River Terek like the sound of a wind in the forest, the impetuous stream rushing between white crusts of frozen foam and washing greenly against ice-crowned boulders. For sixty miles the road is that of the valley of the Terek. It passes the Redant and then becomes the visible companion of the river, winding with it among the primeval grandeur of its rocks. The Kazbek begins to disappear, hidden by its barrier cliffs—its Kremlin; but for a mile or so its snowy cap remains in sight over the great lopsided, jagged crags. The blue smokes of Balta and red-roofed nestling Dolinadalin rise into the afternoon sky. The road enters the chilling shadow of the Gorge of Jerakhof, and you look back regretfully on the red sunlit strand behind you. The white-framed Terek moves in a grand curve through a broad wilderness of stones and snow. An icy mountain draught creeps from the cleft in the grey cold rocks. On the deserted road the telegraph poles and wires assume that sinister expression which they have in vast and lonely mountain tracts. The opening by which you entered the gorge becomes a purple triangle, and far above you and behind you glimmers the tobacco-coloured sunlit Table Mountain.

The road becomes narrower: on the one hand the river roars among ice-mantled rocks, on the other the black silt continually trickles and whispers. The faint crimson of sunset lights the wan towers of Fortoug, and then one by one the yellow stars come out like lamps over the mountain walls.

Through Russian Central Asia

There are three inns between Vladikavkaz and the Kazbek mountain. I stayed at the second, at Larse, and made my supper with some thirty Georgians, Ossetines, and Russians, workmen on the road and chance travellers. Here I heard many rumours of the commercial destiny of the military road, of the thirty-verst tunnel that it is necessary to make, of the Englishman named Stewart, the "Boss of the Terek"—*Khosaïn Tereka*—who has the contract to supply the whole of the Caucasus with electricity, who will or will not make an electric power station in the shadow of Queen Tamara's castle, needing an artificial waterfall three hundred sazhens high.

"But the project has grown cold," said I.

"It will come to nothing," say the hillmen; "for ten years people have been talking of such things, but nothing has changed except that we have got poorer."

But the host is an optimist. "It will come. There will be a tramway from the city to the Kazbek. The trams will go past my door. We shall have electric light and electric cooking, and will become rich."

We remained all thirty in one room all night—square-faced, gentle, sociable Russians in blouses; tall, Roman-looking Georgians and Ossetines in long cloaks, with daggers at their tight waists, with high sheepskin hats on their heads. They ate voraciously bread and cheese and black pigs'-liver, putting the waste ends when they had finished into the bags of their winter hoods—astonishing people to look at, these Caucasians; though half-starved, yet of great stature and iron strength, with fine, broad-topped, intelligent heads, deeply lined, cunning brows, long, beak-like, aquiline noses. They would make splendid soldiers—but not so good "soldiers of industry." They are a people who often fail when they go to America. They all knew men who had gone there and had returned with stories of unemployment or exploitation. Scarcely one of them had a good word to say of America. They all, however, looked forward to the time when the Caucasus would be developed on American lines and hum with Western prosperity. We slept on the tables of the inn, on the bar, in the embrasures of the windows, on the forms, on sacking on the floor—the kerosene lamp was turned low, and nearly everyone snored.

We were all up before dawn, and I accompanied an Ossetine miller who was in search of flint for his mill, and we entered the Gorge of Dariel whilst the stars were dim in the sky. It was a sharp wintry morning, and as the road led ever upward and became ever narrower, the wind was piercing. The leaking rocks of summer where often I had made my morning tea were now grown old in the winter, and had wisps of grey hair hanging down—yard-long icicles and thick tangles of ice. The precipitously falling streams and waterfalls were ice-marble stepping-stones from the Terek to the mountain-top.

We entered the gorge by the little red bridge which, like a brace, unites the two sides of the river at its narrowest point. The stars disappeared. Somewhere the sun was rising, but his light was only in the sky so far above. We beheld the green, primeval ruin of Nature, the red-brown, grey, and green boulders of Dariel in varied immensity and diversity of shape, the vast shingly, boulder-strewn wastes, the adamantine shoulders of porphyry, the cold, ponderous immensities of rock held over the daring little road, the river eddics springing like tigers over the central ledges between fastnesses of ice.

My Ossetine picked up various stones and struck them with his dagger to see how well they sparked, and, having apparently found what he wanted, accepted a lift in an ox-cart and returned back to the inn at Larse. Perhaps it was too cold for him. I walked up to the square cliff of Tamara and the tooth of the wall of the ancient castle where Queen Tamara treacherously entertained strangers, making love to them and feasting them, and then having them murdered; the castle where the devil once arrived in the guise of such an unlucky wanderer—the scene of the story of Lermontof's "Demon."

This was once the frontier of Asia, and the romantic country of a fine fighting people. To this day, despite railway projects and the hope that the river may provide the Caucasus with electricity, Queen Tamara's castle remains almost the newest thing. It is modern beside the antiquity and majesty of the ruin of Nature. Here the real world seems to jut out through the green turf and flower-carpeted earth into the light of day, striking us awfully, like the apparition of God the Father coming up out of the bowers of Eden. You feel yourself in the presence of something even older than mankind itself, and you wonder what differences you would note if, with the goloshes of Fortune on your feet, you could be transported back a thousand years, a second thousand, a third thousand, and so on. What did the Ancients make of this? They held that it was to the Kazbek mountain that Prometheus was bound as a punishment for stealing fire from heaven. Was that what they said when they first came fearfully through and discovered the plains of the North?

An ancient way! And then at the turn of it, the gate to the "Kremlin" of Dariel, and the towering Kazbek lifting itself to the sky within. Here is truly one of the most wonderful and romantic regions in the world. But it was not to see the Kazbek that I made this journey, but to find again a certain cave where years ago I found my companion on the road, the place where we lived and slept by the side of the river. It was there as I left it, familiar, calm, by the side of the running river, glittering in the noonday sun, and the granite boulders held threads of ice and ice-pearls—the ear-rings of the rocks. And I would have liked to meet my companion again. But Heaven knew under what part of its canopy the tramp was wandering then. I felt a home-sickness to be tramping again, and I decided that as soon as the snow and ice had gone I would take to the road.

* * * * *

And so, the season having changed, and the cold winds and rains of spring giving way to summer, I take the road once more into new country. The season really changes when it is possible to sleep comfortably out of doors. This year I go into the depths of the Russian East, and, besides taking the adventures of the road, continue my study of Easternism and Westernism in the Tsar's Empire. I travel by train to Tashkent, the limit of the railway, and then take the road, with my pack on my back, through the deserts of Sirdaria and the Land of the Seven Rivers towards the limits of Chinese Tartary and Pamir, then along the Chinese frontier, north to the Altai mountains and the steppes of Southern Siberia. This is a long, new journey—new for English experience—because, until our entente with Russia, mutual jealousy about the Indian frontier made it extremely difficult for the Russian Government to permit observant and adventurous Englishmen to wander about as I intend to do. Indeed, even now I may be stopped and turned back from some forlorn spot seven or eight hundred miles from a railway station, and then, perhaps, silence may engulf my correspondence for a time. All things may happen; my papers may be confiscated or lost in the post, or my progress may be stopped by various accidents. In any case, I have official permission for my journey, and the weather is fine.

The old grandmother baked me a box of sweet cheesecakes (*vatrushki*), Vassily Vassilitch brought me fruit and chocolate, another friend brought three dozen cabbage pies—thus one always starts out for the wilderness. We assembled in the grandmother's sitting-room to say good-bye. I am to beware of earthquakes, of snakes, of having much money on my person, of being bitten by scorpions, of tigers, wolves, bears, of occult experiences.

"It is occult country," said G——, teacher of mathematics in the "Real School." "You are likely to have occult adventures; some enormous catacylsm is going to take place this summer. I don't know what it is, but I should advise you to get across this dangerous country as soon as you can. Siberia is safe, and North Russia, but not Central Asia, and not, as a matter of fact, Germany."

He had had a strange dream, and, being of occult preoccupation, ventured on vague prophecy, which generally took the form of earthquakes and catacylsms. When I met him in the autumn after my journey, the great war with Germany had broken out, and I was inclined to credit him with a true prophecy; but, with honest wilfulness, he was still figuring out earthquakes and cataclysms to be, and would not have it that the European conflagration was the fulfilment of his dream.

Another friend is charmed with the idea that I am going to Bokhara, and won't I bring her home a silk scarf from the great bazaars? Another is touched by the dream that I am realising. To him Central Asia is a fairyland, and the Thian Shan mountains are not real mountains so much as mountains in a book of legends.

At last the old grandmother says:

"All sit down!"

And we sit, and are silent together for a few

moments, then rise and turn to the Ikon and cross ourselves. The grandmother marks me in the sign of the Cross and blesses me, praying that I may achieve my journey and come safely back, that no harm may overtake me, and that I may have success. Then I pass to each of the others present and say "Good-bye." Vera, however, looks at me in such a way that I am sure she means that she feels I shall never return. So I am bound to ask myself: Is not this farewell a final farewell? Does not this Russian see something that is going to happen to me? But she has been very kind to me, and just at parting puts a beautiful Ikon-print into my hand, and I fix it in the inside of the cover of my stiff map.

* * * * *

The train from Vladikavkaz wanders along the northern side of the Caucasus, unable to find a pass over the mountains. The meadows as far as eye can see are yellowed with cowslips. Now and then a derrick tells that you are in the oil region, and in an hour or so the train steams into the pavement-shed station that marks the weariness and mud of Grozdny, capital of the North Caucasian oilfields. There is a breath of salt air at Petrovsk, a few hours later, and you realise that you have reached the Caspian shore. All night long the train runs along to Baku, glad, as it were, to turn south at last and get round the Caucasus it cannot cross. At Baku I change and take steamer across the Caspian Sea to Krasnovodsk, on the salt steppes, but I have a whole day to wait in the city.

Ordinarily, you come to Baku to make money.

There is nothing to tempt you there otherwise. In windy weather you are blinded with clouds of flying sand; in the heat of summer you are stifled with kerosene odours. It is a commercial city without glamour. Though it boasts several millionaires and is an important name in every financial newspaper in the world, it has no public works, nothing by virtue of which it can take its stand as a Western city. The working men are very badly paid—that is, according to our Western standards—and they do not obtain the few advantages of industrial civilisation that ought to come to make up for dreary life and health lost. There is a constant ferment amongst the labouring classes in the city, and repeated strikes, even in war time. Baku, again, is one of the last refuges of the horse tram and the kerosene street-lamp. It is only in the eastern quarter that the town has charm. There you may see strings of camels loping up the steep streets, panniers on their worn, furry backs, Persians squatting between the panniers, contentedly bobbing up and down with the movement of the beast. Or you may watch the camels kneeling to be loaded, crying appealingly as the heavy burdens are put on them, cumbrously lifting themselves again, hind-legs first, and joining the waiting knot of camels already loaded.

The great shopping place—the bazaar—is wholly Eastern, and even more characteristic than in Russia proper. I feel how the bazaar and the ways of the bazaar came to Russia from the East. As you go from stall to stall you are besieged by porters holding empty baskets—they want to be hired to walk behind you and carry your purchases as you make them. Characters of the Arabian Nights, these; and yet in the streets of Warsaw and Kief, and many other cities, those men in red hats and brass badges, who sit on the kerb or on doorsteps waiting for passers-by to hire them, are really the lineal Westernised descendants of the tailor's fifth brother—I think it was the fifth brother who was a porter.

In the harbour, at the pier where my boat is waiting, I watch the Persian dockers working. Real slaves they are, working twelve hours a day for 1s. 4d. (60 copecks). They have straw-stuffed pack carriers on their backs, like the saddling of camels, and the rhythm of their movement as they proceed with their burdens from the warehouse to the ship is that of slavery. The name of slavery has gone, but the fact remains. Still, the European is not awakened to pity. The Persians are the human camels, work hardest of all the people of the East, and are the least discontented. They are singing and crying and calling all the time they work. The East slaves for the West, but still is not much influenced by the West. It is not they who cause the strikes.

Just before the time for my boat to leave another boat arrives from Lenkoran, and out of it come a party of Persian men with carpet bags slung across their shoulders, their wives in black veils, many-coloured cloaks, and baggy cotton trousers, their children all carrying earthenware pots. More labour available on the docks, more homes occupied in the little houses that dot the eight-mile crescent of the mountainous city of Baku.

The boat leaves at nightfall. It is the *Skobelef*, a handsome steamer, built in Antwerp in 1902. It must have been brought to the Caspian along the waterways of Europe; an officer on board ventures the opinion that it was brought to Baku in parts and fitted up there. A pleasant ship, however it was brought—considerably superior to the ordinary American lake-steamer, for instance. There were very few passengers, and these lay down to sleep at once, fearing the storm that was blowing, so I remained alone on deck and watched the retreating shore. Leaving Europe for America, you sit up in the prow and look ahead, over the ocean; at least, you do not sit and watch the Irish coast disappear. But leaving Europe for Asia, you sit aft and watch her to the last. And the retreating lights of Baku are the lights of Europe.

The night is very dark and starless, and so the eight-mile semicircle of lights is wonderful to behold; the handsome lanterns of the pier, the lights of the esplanade, of the three variety theatres, of the cinemas and shops, the thousands of sparks of homes on the mountain-side. This is the real beginning of my journey, and it is very thrilling; good to sit in the wind and feel the movement of the sea; good to watch the many lighthouses turning red, then green, in the night, and to pass within ten yards of a little lamp, just over the surface of the sea, alternately going out and bursting into brightness every thirty seconds. The lamp seems to say : " There is danger . . . there is danger," and it whispers joyful intelligence to the heart.

There is trouble on the water as we reach the open sea, and the boat begins to roll, but it is still pleasant on the upper deck, and the high wind is warm.

The lights of Baku and Europe have been gradually erased. First to go were the sparks of the homes on the mountain-side, then the lights of the esplanade; the eight great lamps of the pier remain, and one by one they disappear till there is only the great yellow-green flasher that tells ships coming into the harbour just where Baku is. That also disappears at last, and it begins to rain heavily. So I go down to my berth to sleep.

Next morning the wide green sea was sunlit and flecked with white crests of turning waves. Looking out of a port-hole, I saw the bright light of morning shining on the grey and accidental-looking mountains of Asia. The boat was coming into Krasnovodsk.

II

WHERE THE DESERT BLOSSOMS

KRASNOVODSK is one of the hottest, most desert, and miserable places in the world. The mountains are dead; there is no water in them. Rain scarcely ever falls, and the earth is only sand and salt. Strange that even there there is a season of spring, and little shrubs peep forth in green and live three weeks or a month before they are finally scorched up. I spent the day with a kind Georgian to whom I had a letter; a shipping agent at the harbour. He was to have helped me, supposing the local *gendarmerie* should stop my landing. But by an amusing chance I escaped the inspecting officer's attention, and got into Trans-Caspia without questions or passport-showing. One can never be quite sure of passing, even when one's papers are in order. The Russian Government does not give a written passport for Central Asia, but transmits your name to all the local authorities, and you have to trust, first, to their having received your name and, second, to their agreeing that the name received in its Russian spelling is the same as yours written in English on your British passport. In the case of a name such as mine, which is spelt one way and pronounced another, there is likely to be difficulties. During my stay in Central

Asia, moreover, I saw my name spelt in the following cheerful ways—Grkhazkn, Groyansk, and, of course, the inevitable Graggam, and on some occasions I had the difficult task of persuading Russian officials that the names were one and the same. Still, they were inclined to be lenient.

The Georgian was very hospitable; he took me from the pier to his house, behind six or seven wilted and tired acacia trees, gave me a bedroom, bade the samovar and coffee for me; and I made my breakfast and then slept the three hot hours of the day. In the evening he brought up his other Caucasian compatriots from the settlement, a little band of exiles, and we talked many hours to the tune of the humming samovar. We talked of Vladikavkaz and the Kazbek beloved of Georgians, and of my tramps and of mutual acquaintances in Caucasian towns and villages, talked of ethics and politics, and the working man, and of Russia, especially of modern Russia, with its bourgeois and the evil town life. Mine host had almost Victorian-English sentiments, did not like the slit skirt and Tango stocking—so evident in Baku, did not know what women were coming to—despised the Russians for their flirting and dancing and gay living, believed in quiet family life as the foundation of personal happiness, and in Socialism as the foundation of political blessedness. The lights of Europe had not quite disappeared.

As the train did not leave till twelve, we had a long and pleasant evening, and when the time came to go mine host brought me a big bottle of Kakhetian wine, and we all went together to the railway station. I got my ticket, found my carriage. No commotion, no excitement, the empty midnight train crept out of the station, over the salt steppes, and I felt as if in the whole long train there was only myself. It was very vexatious, leaving in the shadow of dark night when no landscape was visible, but there was consolation in the fact that the train accomplished no more than seventy-five miles before sunrise. Next morning, directly I awakened, I looked out of the train, and there before my gaze was the desert; yellow-brown sand as far as eye could see, and on the horizon the enigmatical silhouette of a string of camels, looking like a scrap of Eastern handwriting between earth and heaven. A new sight in front of me, for I had never seen the desert before, except, of course, in Palestine, where it is hardly characteristic. The cliffs of Krasnovodsk had disappeared; the desert was on either hand. I looked in vain for a house or a tree anywhere, but I saw again, as at Krasnovodsk, Nature's pathetic little effort to make a home—an occasional yellow thistle in bloom, a wan pink in blossom here and there on the sand. The train was going so slowly that it seemed possible to step down on to the plain, pick a flower, and return.

Strange that the Russian Government should take railways over the desert before it has developed its home trade routes! The Western mind would find this railway almost inexplicable. You might almost take it to be an elaborate game of make-believe. The train is scheduled in the time-table among the fast trains, and yet at successive empty desert stations stops 21, 31, 14, 6, 12, 12 minutes respectively, and takes 23 hours to traverse the 390 miles from Krasnovodsk to Askhabad, an average rate of 17 miles an hour. The reason for this slowness lies, perhaps, in the fact that the sleepers are not very well laid, and would be dislodged if greater speed were attempted; and the stops at the stations are impressive, indulge a Russian taste for getting out of trains and having a look round, and also, incidentally, let the wild natives know that the steam caravan is waiting for them if they want to go. We stop longer at one of these blank desert stations than the Nord express at Berlin or a Chicago express at Niagara. Russia is not excited about loss of time. Time may be money in America; it is only copper money in Russia, and it is more interesting to have a political railway across the deserts of Asia than to help the fruit-growers of Abkhasia or to functionise industrially the vast railwayless North.

It is dull travelling, but hills at length appear—the lesser Balkans, the greater Balkans; salt marshes give way to sandbanks—drifts of sand heaped up and shaped by the wind like grey snowdrifts. The beautiful curving lines of the sandbanks are wind runes. All this district was once the bed of the Caspian Sea, or, rather, of an ocean which, it is surmised, stretched on the one hand to beyond the Aral Sea, and on the other to the Azof and the Black Sea. The mountains were islands or shores or dangerous rocks in the sea.

When we had passed the Balkans the country

THE CENTRAL ASIAN RAILWAY: NEARING THE OXUS

improved *by bits.* Suddenly, far away, a patch of green appeared, and one's eye hailed it as one at sea hails land. When the train drew nearer there came into view a wonderful emerald square thick with young wheat, set in the absolute grey and brown of the wilderness. This was the first irrigated field. Soon a second and a third field appeared in blessed contrast and refreshment. Out of the yellowish, cloudy sky the sun burst free, and I remembered that it was the first of May. So May Day commenced for me.

People began to appear at the stations, which up till then had been desolate; stately Turkomans, wearing from shoulders to ankles red and white *khalati*, bath-robes rather than dresses; Tekintsi, in hats of white, brown or black sheepskin, hats as big and bigger than the bearskins of our Grenadiers; fat, broad-lipped Kirghiz, with Mongolian brows and rat-tail moustachios drooping to their close-cropped beards; poor Bactrian labourers, in many colours; rich Persian merchants, in sombre black. Many women stood at the stations with hot, just-boiled eggs, with roast chickens, milk or koumis in bottles, even with pats of butter, with samovars. And there were native boys with baskets heaped full of *lepeshki* (cakes of bread). Each station was provided with a long barrier, and the women, in lines of twenty or thirty, stood behind their wares and cried to the passengers. The many steaming samovars were a welcome sight, and at the charge of a halfpenny I made myself tea at one of them.

The country steadily improved, and the train passed by fields along whose every furrow little artificial streams were trickling, past many more emerald wheatfields surrounded by big dykes. The yellow dust of this desert needs only water to make it abundantly fertile; it is not merely frayed rock and stone, as the sand of the seashore, but an organic substance which has been settling from the atmosphere for ages—the *lessovaya zemlya.* When we realise that there is of this strange dust a coat deep enough to be a soil, we understand something of the antiquity of the desert and the fact that, when we consider geological history, our mind must range over millions of years, whereas in thinking of the history of man we are almost aghast to think of thousands of years. So the *leoss* dust settles out of the clear air. Incidentally, what else may not be settling out of the air into the everyday of our world? The spring flowers show the richness of this dust of the wilderness, for now behold the desert under the influence of irrigation blooming as the rose. It does, indeed, actually blosson with the rose, for I notice even on the fringe of the hopeless desert the sweetbriar, and it is unusually lovely. At the new stations little children appear, having in their hands little clusters of deep crimson blossoms. Poppies now appear on the waste, irises, saxifrages, mulleins, toadflax—the voice of a rich country crying in the midst of the sand. Here it is literally true:

> Full many a flower is born to blush unseen,
> And waste its sweetness on the desert air.

By evening the train is running along the frontier of the north of Persia, and every house has a garden of

THE CENTRAL ASIAN DESERT

roses. A Persian silk merchant, all in black, with a talisman of green jade hanging from a gold chain round his neck, comes into my carriage, and prepares to occupy the upper shelf. He is travelling all night to Merv, and has brought a great bouquet of sweet-smelling, double roses into the carriage. A knobbly-nosed, grey-faced, animal-eared, antediluvian old sort, this Persian would not stay in my carriage because there was a woman in it, but asked me to keep his place while he went and locked himself in the empty women's compartment next door. He left his black, horn-handled, slender, leather-wrapped walking-stick behind—its ferrule was of brass, and seven inches long.

We reached Geok-Tepe, a great fortress of the Tekintsi, reduced by Skobelef in 1881. At the railway station there is a room in which are preserved specimens of all the weapons used in the fight. There are also waxwork representations of a Russian soldier with his gun, and a native soldier cutting the air with his semi-circle of a sword. Many passengers turned out to have a look at these things. It was sunset time, and the west was glowing red behind the train, the evening air was full of health and fragrance, the stars were like magnesium lights in the lambent heaven, the young moon had the most wonderful place in the sky, poised and throned not right overhead, but some degrees from the zenith, as it were on the right shoulder of the night.

It was an evening that touched the heart. At every station to Askhabad the passengers descended from the train, and walked up and down the platforms and talked. The morning of May Day had been blank and dismal; the evening was full of gaiety and life. We reached Askhabad, the first great city of Turkestan, about eleven o'clock at night, and its platform presented an extraordinary scene. The whole forty-five minutes of our stay it was crowded with all the peoples of Central Asia—Persians, Russians, Afghans, Tekintsi, Bokharese, Khivites, Turkomans—and every one had in his hand, or on his dress, or in his turban roses. The whole long pavement was fragrant with rose odours. Gay Russian girls, all in white and in summer hats, were chattering to young officers, with whom they paraded up and down, and they had roses in their hands. Persian hawkers, with capacious baskets of pink and white roses, moved hither and thither; immense and magnificent Turkomans lounged against pillars or walked about, their bare feet stuck into the mere toe-places they call slippers—they, too, held roses in their fingers. In the third-class waiting-room was a line of picturesque giants waiting for their tickets, and kept in order meanwhile by a cross little Russian gendarme. Behind the long barrier, facing the waiting train, stood the familiar band of women with chickens and eggs, with steaming samovars and bottles of hot milk. They had now candle lanterns and kerosene lamps, and the light glimmered on them and on the steam escaping from the boiling water they were selling. I walked out into the umbrageous streets, where triple lines of densely foliaged trees cast shadow between you and the beautiful night sky; in depths of dark greenery lay the houses of the city, with grass growing on their far-projecting roofs, with verandas on which the people sleep, even in May. But they were not asleep in Askhabad. I stopped under a poplar and listened to the sad music of the Persian pipes. In these warm, throbbing, yet melancholy strains the night of North Persia was vocal—the night of my May Day.

I returned to the station and bought a large bunch of pink and white roses, and, as the second bell had rung, got back to my carriage, laid my plaid and my pillow, and as the train went out I slipped away from the wonderful city—to a happy dream.

III

WONDERFUL BOKHARA

THE promise of Persia was not fulfilled on the morrow after my train left Askhabad. We turned north-east, and passed over the lifeless, waterless waste of Kara-Kum, 100 miles of tumbled desert and loose sand. At eleven in the morning the temperature was 80 in the shade—each carriage in the train was provided with a thermometer—and the air was charged with fine dust, which found its way into the train despite all the closed windows and closed doors. Through the window the gaze ranged over the utmost disorder—yellow shores, all ribbed as if left by the sea, sand-smoking hillocks, hollows specked with faint grasses where the marmot occasionally popped out of sight. At one point on the passage across we came to mud huts, with Tekintsi standing by them, and to a reach of the desert where a herd of ragged-looking dromedaries were finding food where no other animal would put its nose. Then we passed away into uninterrupted flowerless sandhills, all yellow and ribbed by the wind. So, all the way to the red Oxus River. It is called the Amu-Darya now, but it is the ancient Oxus, a fair, broad stream at Chardzhui, but, from its colour, more like a river of red size than of water. All the canals and dykes of the irrigation system of the district flow with the red water of the river, and wherever the water is conducted the desert blossoms like virgin soil. The river is the sun's wife, and the green fields are their children.

Chardzhui, the port on the Oxus, is the point for embarkation for Khiva. There is a small fleet of Government steamers plying between the two cities, though it is comparatively difficult for travellers on private business to obtain a passage on one of them. When first this fleet was started there was some idea that Russia would use them in her imperial warfare as she pushed south, but probably the vessels have little military significance nowadays. For the rest, Chardzhui is famous for its melons, which grow to the size of pumpkins and are very sweet. Frequently in Petrograd shops or in fashionable restaurants one may see enormous melons hanging from straps of bast—these are the fruits of Chardzhui. At this season of the year Chardzhui has a great deal of mud and does not invite travellers, especially as its inns are bad.

The train entered the Russian Protectorate of Bokhara, and the population changed. From Askhabad the natives had special cattle-trucks afforded them, and they sat on planks stretched over trestles; they were Sarts, Bokharese, Jews, Afghans. Into my carriage came two Mohammedan scholars going to Bokhara city. They washed their hands, spread carpets on one side of the carriage, knelt on the other, said their prayers, prostrated themselves. Then they took out a copy of the Koran, and one read to the other in a sonorous and poetical voice all the way to the city,—they were Sarts, a very ancient tribe of Aryan extraction, some of the finest-looking people of Central Asia, tall, dignified, wrinkled, wearing gorgeous cloaks and snowy turbans. The two in my carriage had, apparently, several wives in another compartment, as they each carried a sheaf of tickets. The women hereabout were very strictly in their *charchafs*. There was no peeping out or peering round the corner, such as one sees in Turkey, but an absolute black, blotting out of face and form. When you looked at five or six sitting patiently side by side, each and all in voluminous green cloaks, and where the faces should appear a black mask the colour and appearance of an oven-shelf, you felt a horror as if the gaze had rested on corpses or on the plague-stricken.

From the Oxus valley the people swarmed in a populous land, and it was a sight to see so many Easterns drinking green tea from yellow basins. Already we were nearer China than Russia, and the sight took me back in memory to Chinatown, New York, and the *chop suey* restaurants. I fell into conversation with a Tartar merchant in carpets, and I tried to obtain an idea of what Bokhara was like in the year of grace 1914.

"Is there an electric tramway in Bokhara, or a horse tramway?"

"No, nothing of the sort. The streets are so narrow, two carts can't pass one another without collision."

"Are there any hotels?"

"There are caravanserai."

"No European buildings?"

"Only outside the town. There is a Russian police-station, and a hotel built for officials. The Emir won't allow any hotels to be built within the walls."

At length we reached New Bokhara, the Russian town, with its white houses, avenues of trees, its broad streets, and shops, and we changed to a by-line for Ancient Bokhara. The train drew through pleasant meadows and cornfields, bright and fertile as the South of England, and after twelve sunny versts we came into view of the cement-coloured mud walls of the most wonderful city of Mohammedan Asia, a place that might have been produced for you by enchantment—that reminds you of Aladdin's palace as it must have appeared in the desert to which the magician transported it. Within toothed walls—a grey Kremlin eight miles round—live 150,000 Mohammedans, entirely after their own hearts, without any appreciable interference from without, in narrow streets, in covered alleys, with endless shops, behind screening walls. The roads are narrow and cobbled, and wind in all directions, with manifold alleys and lanes, with squares where stand handsome mosques, with portals and stairways leading down to the cool and tree-shaded, but stagnant, little reservoirs that hold the city's water. Along the roadway various equipages come prancing—muddy *proletkas*, unhandy-looking, egg-shaped carts, with clumsy wooden wheels eight feet high, and projecting axles, gilt and crimson-covered carts made of cane and straw, the shape of a huge egg that has had both ends sliced off. The Bek, or

Bokharese magistrate, comes bounding along in his carriage, with outriders, and all others give him salute as he passes. It is noticeable that the drivers of vehicles prefer to squat on the horses rather than sit in drivers' seats. Strings of laden camels blunder on the cobbles, innumerable Mohammedans come, mounted on asses—it is clear that man is master when you see an immense Bokharese squatting on a meek ass and holding a huge cudgel over its head. Charchaffed women are even seen on asses, and some of them carry a child in front of them. There are continually deadlocks in the narrow lanes, and all the time the drivers shout "*Hagh, hagh!*" ("Get out of the way, get out of the way!")

The houses are made of the ruins of bygone houses, of ancient tiles and mud. They have fine old doors of carven wood, but no windows looking on the streets. A sort of inlaid cupboard, with a glass window, half open, a spread of wares, and a Moslem sitting in the midst, is a shop. Thus sits the vendor of goods, but also the maker—the tinsmith at work, the coppersmith, the maker of hats. The bazaars are rich and rare, and in the shadow of the covered streets—there are fifty of them—the lustrous silks and carpets, and pots and slippers, in the shops each side of the way, have an extraordinary magnificence; the gorgeous vendors, sitting patiently, not asking you to buy, staring at the heaps of metallics, silver-bits and notes resting on the little tabourets in front of them, belong to an age which I thought was only to be found in books. What a wealthy city it is! It offers more silks and carpets for

BOKHARA: THE ESCORT OF A MAGISTRATE

sale than London or Paris; it is an endless warehouse of covetable goods.

What strikes you at Jerusalem or Constantinople is the abundance of English goods for sale, but here at Bokhara there is a strange absence of Western commodities. Formerly the English sent all sorts of manufactures by the caravan road from India, but since the Russians ringed round their Customs system the commercial influence of England has waned. Western goods come via Russia. What European articles there are come from Germany or Scandinavia. For the rest, as in other Eastern cities, the street arabs hawk churek-cakes and *lepeshki;* men in white sit at corners selling, in this case, *Bokharese* delight, brown twists of toffee, old-fashioned sugar-candy which in piles looks like so much rock crystal. Beggars in rags sit outside the mosques and hold up to you Russian basins—they do not, however, cry and clamour and follow you, as in the tourist-visited cities of Asia Minor and North Africa. Outside every other shop is a bird-cage and a large pet bird; in some cases falcons, much prized in these lands. I admired the falcons, and their owners seemed childishly pleased at the attention I gave them. I gave a piece of Bokharese silver to a beggar outside a mosque (the Bokharese have their own silver coinage, which, however, looks like ancient coin rather than any which is now in use). In one of the big shadowy bazaars I bought a delicious silk scarf of old-rose colour full of light and loveliness, falling into a voluminous grandeur as the melancholy Eastern showed it me. I did not bargain about its price, that seemed almost impossible, only five roubles (ten shillings), and the lady who has it now says it is enough to make a whole robe. Somehow I liked it better as a scarf than I could if it were "made up."

I passed out of the city and walked round the walls. A road encompasses them, and on the road are camels with blue beads on their necks and many Easterns riding them. There is a strange feeling of contrast in being outside the city. The arc of the grey walls goes gradually round and away from you, surrounding and enclosing the life of the city; the city is like a magical box full of strange magicians and singers and toy shop-men and customers; it is like a strange human beehive full of life. And outside the walls there is the sudden contrast of fresh air and space and life and greenery and broad sky. Inside the city the streets are so narrow that you feel the "box" has got the lid on. Someone said to me when I went to New York: "We'll give you the freedom of the city with the lid off." Well, Bokhara has the lid *on*. And you feel that certainly when you get outside and look at the silent, significant enclosing wall. But the fields are deep in verdure, and it is like a lovely June day in England—the willow leaning lovingly over you, overwhelmed with leaves. The walls are battlemented, rent, patched up, buttressed; there are eleven gates, and at each gate the traffic going in and out has a processional aspect. Along the walls, between gate and gate, there is a deep and gentle peace. No sound comes through the walls; they are broad and high and solid. The swallows nesting there twitter. You cannot obtain a glimpse, even of the high mosques within.

I entered the city once more, lost myself in its mazes, and was obliged to take a native cab in order to get out again. I was living outside the town in an inn specially built for men on Government service. I got the last empty room. Pleasant it was to lie back in the sun and be carried along twenty wonderful streets and lanes, seeing once more all I had seen before of colour and Orientalism.

The Bokharese are a gentle people. They wear no weapons. They sit in the grass market and chatter and smile over their basins of tea. The little pink doves of the streets search between their bare feet for crumbs. The wild birds of the desert build in the walls of their houses and bazaars. On the top of the tower of every other mosque is an immense storks' nest, overlapping the turret on all sides. Some of these nests must be eight to ten feet high; they are round, and so look like part of the design of the architecture. Storks are encouraged to build there by the Mohammedans, by whom they are held sacred. It is pleasant to watch the bird itself, standing on one leg, a black but living and moving silhouette against the sky; to listen to the clatter of bills when the father stork suddenly flies down to a nest with food.

Bokhara is a sort of Mussulman perfection—there is no progress to be obtained there except after the destruction of old forms. The Bokharese keep to the forms of their religion and its ethical laws; they wear their clothes correctly; they know their crafts. They are a great contrast to the Russians, who are careless and inexact, and in their worship often nonchalant to their God; to the Russians, who wear nothing correctly and come out in almost any sort of attire; to the Russians, so ignorant and clumsy in their crafts. Yet Russia has all before her, and Bokhara has all behind her.

The Bokharese have no ambition; civilisation and mechanical progress do not tempt them. They have a happy smile for everything that comes along, but nothing moves them. A Russian motor-car comes bounding over the cobbles, whooping and coughing its alarm signals; a score of dogs try to set on it and bite it as it passes, and the natives sit in their cupboard shops and laugh. If the car stops, they do not collect round it, as would a village of Caucasian tribesmen, for instance. There was one Bokharian—a Sart, in full cloak and turban—who rode a bicycle, an astonishing exception.

The Russians at present hold Bokhara very lightly, but will no doubt tighten their hands on it later, as they are taking the solidification of their Central Asian Empire very seriously. At present there are no passports, and there is mixed money; but passports are coming in, and the banks are taking up all the ancient Sartish bits they can get and giving Russian silver in exchange. There are several Russian banks within the city walls, and they have a great influence. The Emir is friendly towards Russia, and is a pompous figure at the Russian Court, though it is rumoured that in his

OUTSIDE ONE OF THE MOST FAMOUS OF THE MOSQUES

native palaces he whiles the long empty day away by playing such elementary card games as *durak*, snap, and happy family. The Russians have permission to build schools in the city, and the Russian bricklayer is to be seen at work with trowel and line, whilst the native navvy carries the hod to and fro. The foreign goods in the bazaar are mostly cotton, and if you examine the splendidly gay prints that go to form the clothing of the natives you find it is all marked Moscow manufacture. The Bokharese merchants go to Nizhni Fair not only to sell, but to buy. There are no English in the streets, no tourists, no Americans. Indeed, I asked myself once in wonder: Where are the Americans? The only people in Western attire are commercial travellers (*commerçants*), and they are mostly Russians or Armenians, though Germans are occasionally to be seen. I noticed knots of these men discussing prices of horse-hair, wool, oil-cake, carpets, silks. It should be remembered that that district is more justly famous for its carpets than for its silks. The best carpets in the world are made by the Tekintsi. Armenians, Turcomans and Persians work in whole villages and settlements in Trans-Caspia making carpets with needle and loom. They have the original tradition of carpet-making, a sense for the particular art of weaving those wonderful patterns of Persia, and for them a carpet is not a covering on which it could be possible to imagine a man walking with muddy boots; it is for dainty naked feet in the harem, or it is a whole picture to be hung on a wall, not thrown on the floor. Singer's sewing machines are, of course, installed at Bokhara; they are in every town in the wide world. The cinema also has come, and a green poster announces that the Tango will be shown after the presentation of a striking comedy called "The Suffragette."

But what does this really matter? Let us ask the deliberate stork, standing on one leg on the height of the mosque of Lava-Khedei. The mosque tower has a clock, and the stork seems to be trying to read the time. But he will give no answer, nor will the Mussulmans below; they also are scanning the wall to see if it is nearer the hour to pray. And the clock, be it observed, is not set by Petrograd time.

IV

MOHAMMEDAN CITIES AND MOHAMMEDANISM

THE consideration of the wonderful Moslem cities, Constantinople, Cairo, Jerusalem and Bokhara, with their marvellous blending of colours, their characteristic covered ways and bazaars, their great spreads of lace and silk and carpets, slippers, fezes, turbans, copper ware, their gloomy stone ways and close courts, their blind houses, made windowless that their women be not seen, their great mosques and splendid tombs, inevitably suggests a great question of the East. What is Mohammedanism, what does it mean? At Cairo and Jerusalem, and even at Constantinople, it is possible to doubt the real nature of the Moslem world; it seems a makeshift world giving way readily to Western influence, or, in any case, reproved by the more splendid and vital institutions of the West standing side by side with many shabby and wretched phenomena of the East.

But Bokhara is a perfect place. It is much more remote even than Delhi, and is almost untouched, unaffected by Western life. It is a city of a dream, and if a magician wished to transport some modern Aladdin to a fairy city, where there would be nothing recognisable and yet everything would be beautiful and bewildering, he need only bring him to the walls of Bokhara. Through Bokhara and its undisturbed peace and beauty, one obtains a new vision of Mohammedanism, and it becomes absurd to think that the real Moslem world is of the same pattern as the Westernised and yet strangely picturesque cities with which we are familiar. We remember the fact that there are so many millions more Mohammedans than there are Christians, that they live off the railways, in deserts, in far away and remote cities, that they journey on camels and in caravans, and that to them their religion and way of life are sufficient, that they do not seek new words or inspiration, nor do they want time to do other things, nor change of any kind. We remember their mystery, their faith and loyalty, their superb detachment, their state of being enough unto themselves, their playfulness, audacity, hospitality, how they shine compared with Christians in the keeping of the conventions of their religion, their punctual piety, their pilgrimages, and, with all that, their fixed and definite inferiority of caste.

Their pilgrimage to Mecca, which we are apt to regard merely as something picturesque, is in reality one of the most mysterious of human processions. From Northern Africa, from Syria, from Turkey and Armenia, from Turkestan, from the Chinese marches (there are even Chinese Mohammedans, the Duncani), from India, from the depths of Arabia and Persia—to Mecca. Through Russia alone there travel annually considerably more Moslems to Mecca than there do Christian pilgrims to Jerusalem; and some of these

A HOLIDAY AT SAMARKAND: BOYS OF THE MILITARY SCHOOL PLAYING AMONG THE RUINS OF THE TOMB OF TAMERLANE

Mohammedan pilgrims are the most outlandish pilgrims. They are illiterate, simple, unremarked. They do not possess minds which could understand our modern Christian missionaries, and Russia, at least, has no desire to proselytise among them. If the peoples of the world could be seen as part of a great design of embroidery on the garment of God, it would probably be seen that Mohammedanism at the present moment is part of the beauty of the pattern and the amazing labyrinthine scheme. It is not a rent, not a disfigurement.

Mahomet and the Mohammedans is not a subject to dismiss, and when we look at those wondrous cities of the East it is worth while remembering that we are looking at a new image and superscription, and are in the presence of people who own a different but none the less true allegiance. As upon one of the planets we might come across a different race that had not had, and could not have, our revelation.

Our prejudice as militant Christians, however, ought necessarily to be against Mohammedans. They have ever been our religious enemies in arms, the Saracens, the Paynim, the Tartar hordes; we are not very amicably disposed to those of our argumentative brothers who, to show their independence of thought, say they prefer Mohammedanism or Buddhism or Confucianism or what not.

In reading Carlyle's "Heroes and Hero-worship" there is a haunting feeling that it was a pity that for the "Hero as Prophet" he chose Mahomet and not Jesus, or that, choosing Mahomet, he had not travelled in Mohammedan countries, investigating his subject more thoroughly and giving a truer picture of the significance of Mohammedanism and of the man who founded it. The Mahomet section of "Heroes" is like a note that does not sound. Reading the lecture over again, one is struck with a new fact about Carlyle —his insularity of intelligence. Despite the fact that he is preoccupied with French and German history, you notice his narrowness of vision, or perhaps it is that the general vision of the world which men have now was not so accessible in his day, and the differences in national psychology now manifest were hidden in obscurity then. Carlyle saw mankind as Scotsmen, and all true religion whatsoever as a sort of Southern Scottish Puritanism. He saw all national destinies in one and the same type, without any conception of fundamental differences of soul. He admired the Germans, and the Germans adopted him and his works. And he disliked the French because so few of them had that "fixity of purpose" and "manliness," "thoroughness," "grim earnestness" of his compatriots. Russia was a very vague country, but Carlyle approved of the Tsar, dimly discerning in him one who must have something in common with Cromwell or Frederick the Great, "keeping by the aid of Cossack and cannon such a vast empire together." And the further his imagination ranges the more do his notions of foreign peoples and races fail to correspond with his patterns of humanity. Among the many other destinies which Carlyle might have had and lived through, one can imagine one wherein he travelled, and found in real life what he sought in museums and libraries. He would have been a wonderful traveller, and would have known and shown more of the verities and mysteries of the world than he was able to do through the medium of history.

Carlyle's Mahomet is an example of old-fashioned visions. It is clear now that this "deep-hearted Son of the Wilderness, with his beaming black eyes and open social deep soul," was not that determined, conscientious British sort of character that he is made out to be, nor has Mohammedanism that Cromwellian earnestness which Carlyle imputed to it.

It is impossible to find in the Moslem soul "the infinite nature of duty," but we would not explain the "gross sensual paradise" and the "horrible flaming hell" of the Mohammedans by saying that to them "Right is to Wrong as life is to death, as heaven to hell. The one must nowise be done, the other in nowise be left undone." Mahomet and Mohammedanism are not explainable in these terms.

Probably the most common assumption in the West is that Mohammedanism does not count. In its adherents it greatly outnumbers Christianity, but not even those who believe that the will of majorities should prevail would recognise the Mohammedan majority. For though more warlike than we, they have not our weapons, and though they are finer physically, they have not our helps to Nature, nor our civilisation, nor our passion. They are apart, they are scarcely human beings in our Western sense of the term, and are negligible. Still, Mohammedanism is an extraordinary portent in the world. The Mohammedans, those many millions, are not merely potential Christians, a set of people remaining in error because our missionary enterprise is not sufficient to bring them to the Light. It is not an accident, or a makeshift religion, but evidently a happy form suitable to the millions who embody it. It is a poetically fitting religion, part of the very fibre of the people who have it, and it cannot easily be got rid of or supplanted.

As enthusiastic Christians we consider the Moslem world with some vexation; some of us even with malice and a readiness to take arms against it. But as pleasure-seeking tourists and worldly men and women, we rather love the Turk and the Arab for his "picturesqueness," for the picturesqueness of his religion. As sportsmen, we love him because he has the reputation of fighting well.

It was with a certain amount of dissatisfaction that I fell into the hands of an Arab guide when I was in Cairo, and was shown, first of all, the picturesque mosques so beloved of tourists—the Mosque of Sultan Hassan, the Alabaster Mosque, and so on. Not the ancient Egyptian remains, which are the most significant thing in Egypt; not the Early Christian ruins, which are most dear to us (the old Christian monasteries which the Copts possess seemed to be known by none), but the mosques made of the stolen stones of the Pyramids and of the tombs, and inlaid with the jewels taken from ikon frames and rood-screens of the first churches of Christianity. And as I listened to the details of the blinding of the architects, the destruction

MOHAMMEDAN TOMBS AND RUINS IN THE YOUNGEST OF THE RUSSIAN COLONIES

of the Mamelukes, the fighting and the robbing, the disparaging thought arose: "They are all a pack of robbers, these Mohammedans."

They are robbers by instinct, and non-progressive not only in life, but in ideas. But they are picturesque, and have given to a considerable portion of the earth's face a characteristic quaintness and beauty. They cannot be dismissed.

Carlyle tries to see some light in the Koran, and fails. Probably the Koran is translated in a wrong spirit or to suit a British taste. But obviously it is meant to be chanted, and it is full of rhythms with which we are unfamiliar, as unfamiliar as we are with the sobbing, plaintive, screaming music that is melody in the Moslem's ears. The soul of the Koran is not like the soul of the Bible, just as the soul of a mediæval Christian city such as Florence or Rome is unlike Khiva or Bokhara or Samarkand, just as the souls of our eager mystical populations are different from the souls of those simple, satisfied and fatalistic people. It is not easy to communicate the difference by words; it is not merely a difference in clothes. It is a difference in the spirit, a difference in the spirit that causes the expression to be different, whether that expression be clothes, or houses, or cities, or way of life, or music, or literature, or prayer. And while our expression changes, theirs remains the same. Our spirit remains the same, theirs remains the same, but only with us does the expression change.

"God is great; we must submit to God," is Mohammedan wisdom. It is in a way a common ground—we must submit. But with the Mohammedan there is a waiting for God's will to be shown, whereas with us rather a divination of it in advance. We are alive to find out what God wills for us. After "Thy will be done!" we put an exclamation mark and rejoice. Mohammedanism is fatalism, but Christianity is not fatalism.

And if fatalism gives a tinge of melancholy to life, especially to an unfortunate life, it still makes life easier. It relieves the soul of care and takes a world of responsibility off the shoulders. The Mohammedan is a care-free being. He has, more than we have, the life of a child.

Consequently, one of the greatest characteristics of Mohammedan people is playfulness. All is play to them. They are playful in their attire, in their business, in their fighting, in their talking. They buy and sell, and make a great game of their buying and selling. They lack "seriousness." They are in no hurry to strike a bargain and get ahead in trade. Their instinct is for the game rather than for the business. Hence the comparative poverty of the Tartars—the most commercial people of the East. They are not serious enough to get rich in our Western way. If they would get really rich as a Western merchant is rich, they must not waste time playing and haggling. They fight well because they see the game in fighting. Death is not so great a calamity to them as to us, for life is not such a serious thing. They look on playfully at suffering, and laugh to see men's limbs blown away by bombs. They like the gamble of modern warfare.

And, of course, they were warriors and robbers before they were Mohammedans. Fighting is one of their deepest instincts, and as they do not change with time as we do, they have an almost anachronistic love of battle. They are fond of weapons as of toys, fingering blades and laughing, guffawing at the sight of cannon. They love steamboats and battleships as children love toy steamboats, and they sail them on the waters of the Levant as children would their toys. Their hospitality is mirthful, as are also their murders and their massacres. Their heaven and hell are playful conceptions.

The condition of their remaining children is obedience to the simple laws of their religion. These obeyed, they are free of all troubles. And they obey. Hence, from Delhi to Cairo and from Kashgar to Constantinople, a playful and sometimes mischievous and difficult world. Looking at the great cities, with their quaint figures and their chaffering, their elfish spires and minarets, their covered ways and gloomy and mysterious passages; looking at this city of Bokhara, with its covered ways crowded with these children-merchants and children-purchasers, their beggars, tombs, shrines, we must remember it is all a children's contrivance, something put together by a people who do not grow up and do not grow serious as we do—mysterious yet simple, fierce yet childlike, valorous and yet amused by suffering, Islam, the enemy of the Church in arms, to this day.

V

THE HISTORY OF THE TRIBES

FROM Bokhara I proceeded to Samarkand, the grave of Timour. Turkestan has four great cities remaining in splendour from the most remote times—Bokhara, Khiva, Samarkand, and Tashkent. Alexander the Great conquered most of this territory and established himself at Samarkand for winter quarters, but there are few traces of Alexander to-day. In his day the land was inhabited by tribes who had come out of the Pamir—Persians, Indians, Tadzhiks. There were also primeval nomads, with their tents and their herds, a people something like the Jews when they were simply the Children of Israel, when they were a *family*. There were possibly hordes of Jews, as there were hordes of Tartars and Mongols. At the time of the shepherd dynasty of Egypt the peoples of the East were living in patriarchal families, resembling in a way the families of the Kirghiz in Central Asia to-day.

For the ethnologist Central Asia is necessarily one of the most interesting districts of the world, and its inhabitants are like living specimens in a great ethnological museum. The races there tell us more about the past of the world in which we are interested than any pages in the history book. Here we may feel what the Children of Israel were, the Egyptians, the Syrians, the Persians, the Turks, the Russians. We see the destiny of Rome, the destiny of the Church of Christ, of Christianity, of barbarism.

Not that there are many pure or clear types of historical races in Central Asia to-day. The land has been a running ground for fierce tribes coming out of China and Manchuria, coming from the mysterious and vague regions of the Pamir and Thibet. The Kirghiz to-day exhibit every shade of difference between the Mongol and the Turk.

After the Greeks of Alexander came the first ferocious Huns. To the Greeks what is now Russia and Siberia, Seven Rivers Land and Russian Central Asia was vaguely Scythia. They fumbled northward and eastward as in a great darkness, and they were rather afraid to go on. Yet we know that even before the records of Greek history there was an Eastern trade on the Volga and from the Caspian to the Baltic. The merchants of Persia and India traded with the Russia of those days. The Persians ruled from the Oxus to the Danube, and in the wilderness stretching from the Oxus to the Great Wall of China dwelt the primeval nomads.

South of the Altai Mountains was the fount of the mysterious Huns who, some centuries before the birth of Christ, ravaged China to the Pacific and extended their dominion northward, down the Irtish River to the *tundra* of the Arctic Circle. These were not a Mongol people, but Turkish, though eventually they were beaten by the Tartars, and the Mongolian and Turkish tended to blend. The reason for their turning westward was an eventual failure against China. The Chinese built their fifteen-hundred-mile wall against the Huns, but the wall did not avail them; they were beaten, and were forced to pay an enormous tribute of silk, gold, and women. Then the Chinese reorganised their armies, turned upon their enemies, and crushed them. Their monarch became a vassal of the Emperor. Fifty-eight hordes entered the service of China—a horde was about four thousand men. The remainder of the Huns, coming to the conclusion that China was too strong for them, resolved to fight somewhere else, and set off westward towards the Oxus and the Volga. They expended themselves on the eastern shores of the Volga, where they remain to this day as the Kalmeeks. Visitors to the Southern Ural and the district of Astrakhan will have pointed out to them the Kalmeeks, a low-browed, broad-nosed type of men, sun-browned, wizened, and squat, the ugliest in Russia; these are the original Huns, ferocious in their day, very peaceful and stupid now, and below even the level of the Kirghiz in intelligence.

The chief Turkish tribes to-day are the Yakuts, on the Lena, the Kirghiz, the Uzbeks, of whom there are a considerable number in Bokhara and Khiva, the Turkomans, and Osmanli, the Turks themselves, and they have all something of the Hun about them. Their history is Hunnish history. A deformed and brutal people were the hordes of the Huns; there were many cripples among them and people of distorted features, many dwarfs. They were the cruellest people that have ever been, and probably that is why they have such a name for ugliness. Cruelty and ugliness of feature go together. Even the most refined torturers of the Spanish Inquisition must have been ugly. There is something terrifying in the aspect of cruelty. It is an aspect of mania, and when it comes out in the race must be called racial mania or aberration.

Successive hordes of pagans rolled forward, and the story of each forward movement of this kind is the same. Each wave, however, seemed to roll farther than the one before and gather in power and volume to the point where it multitudinously broke. The Asiatic heathen were soon over the Volga and across Russia; it was they who set the North German tribes moving and gave an impetus to the plundering and ransacking of the Western world. They astonished even the Goths by their ferocity and ugliness, and in A.D. 376 the Goths had to appeal to the Romans for protection. The Emperor Valens delayed to answer, and a million Goths crossed the Danube and began the conquest of Roman territory. The Huns joined with the Alani, a wild Finnish tribe supposed by some to be the present Ossetini of the Northern Caucasus, and together they obtained glimpses of the splendour of the South and came into touch with the people who would ultimately give them their religion —the Saracens.

Away in the background of Central Asia, however, Mongol tribes were falling on those Huns who had remained behind and ever setting new hordes going westward, and the impact from China was felt all the way to Germany, and hordes of barbarians began to appear before the gates of Rome itself. Soon the Goths burned the capital of the world (A.D. 410). A quarter of a century later the Huns found a new leader in Attila (A.D. 433-453), and became once more the scourge and terror of all existent civilisation. The Huns of Attila were not just the old Huns who came out of Mongolia and fought with the Chinese, but a mixture of all the Turkish tribes of the East. They worshipped the sword, stuck in the ground, and prayed before it as others prayed before the Cross. Attila claimed to have discovered the actual sword of the God Mars, and through the possession claimed dominion over the whole world. He conquered Russia and Germany, Denmark, Scandinavia, the islands of the Baltic. He crushed the Chinese and Tartars who were afflicting the rearguard of his nation in the depths of Asia, negotiating on equal terms with the Emperor of China. He traversed Persia and Armenia and what is now Turkey in Asia, broke through to Syria, and, in alliance with the Vandals, took possession of "Africa." His followers crossed the Mediterranean, devastating the cities of Greece, Italy, and Gaul. Rome abandoned her Eastern Empire to the Huns in A.D. 446; and, after Attila's death, the Vandals, a people of Slavonic origin, sacked Rome once more. Western civilisation seemed to be extinguished, and a barbarian became King of Italy.

What was happening in Central Asia is but vaguely known. The people who lived on the horse at the time of Herodotus still lived on the horse as they do at this day, on mare's milk, koumis, and

A MOHAMMEDAN FESTIVAL AT SAMARKAND—THE HOUR OF PRAYER

horseflesh, camping amidst great herds of horses, the same breed as the Siberian ponies which the Cossacks ride now. There were feuds of the hordes, raids, massacres; the Chinese are said to have attempted to introduce Buddhism, though without much success. There was much intermarriage of Turks and Mongols. On the other hand, the conquering Huns returned with wives of the races of the West, and with a smattering of Western ideas, bringing even with them the name of Christianity, and some Christian ideas. Christians began to appear in the ranks of the pagans.

In the seventh century Mahomet was born, and the characteristic religion of the East took its start, and was soon conquering adherents by the sword; armies of Arabs and Semitic tribes, initiating the propaganda of Islam, conquered Persia, Syria, and portions of Northern Africa and of Spain. In the eighth century they crossed the Oxus, drove hordes of Huns back into the depths of Asia, captured the rich cities of Bokhara and Samarkand, and made Mohammedans of all the people all the way to the Indus. So Uzbeks and Turkomans and Kirghiz and Afghans and the others obtained a religion which suited their temperament, and there was comparative peace and trade throughout all Turkestan and Persia for many a long year. The next great disturbance was caused by the ferment of the Tartars and the mongrel Mongolian Huns, which came to a head under the leadership of Chingiz Khan (A.D. 1206-1227), who was the next conqueror of the world springing out of Asia. He made for himself an enormous empire, extending from the Sea of Japan to the River Nieman in Germany, and from the *tundras* of the Arctic Circle to the wastes of India and Mesopotamia. There were in his army idolaters and Judaic, Mohammedan, and Christian converts. He was the Emperor of the "Moguls"—the word Mogul is the same as Mongol. Among his feats he laid siege to Pekin, and starved the Chinese to such a point that they were forced to kill and eat every tenth man within the city. He conquered Bokhara and Samarkand again, crushed the Russians and the Poles, took Liublin and Cracow, and, at the battle of Lignitz, defeated the Germans, filling nine sacks with the right ears of the slain. Because of Chingiz Khan all Western Europe trembled.

The manners of the hordes of Chingiz Khan and his successors were very like the manners of the old Huns, and they also brought their flocks with them, and lived on roast sheep and roast horse and koumis as the majority of the dwellers of Central Asia seem to have ever lived.

The splendour of the successors of Chingiz Khan decayed, and Russia and the East gasped and waited till Asia produced another monster—a new conqueror of the world. In the fourteenth century he arose, the worst of all, Tamerlane the Great, called Timour the Lame, who conquered everything that had ever been conquered before by Tartar or Hun. Under him Mohammedanism reached a great splendour and came nearest to world-domination.

Both Bokhara and Samarkand fell to Tamerlane.

CENTRAL ASIAN JEWESSES

He conquered great stretches of Persia, Syria, Turkey, the Caucasus, India, Russia and Siberia, besieged Moscow and Delhi in two successive years, dethroned twenty-seven kings, harnessed kings to his chariot instead of horses.

I spent the May of this year in what is particularly the land of Tamerlane, a sort of Russian India on the northern side of Hindu Kush, a country with a majestic past but with little present. Tamerlane the Tartar was once Emperor of Asia, and a potentate of greater fame than Alexander. At the head of the Tartar hordes he conquered all the nations of the East and ravaged every land, committing everywhere deeds of splendour and of barbaric cruelty. The cruelty that is in the Cossack and the Russian, and the taste for barbaric splendour, comes directly from his Tartars. But the greatness of the Tartars has passed away—they are all tradesmen and waiters to-day—and the greatness of the Russians has come about—they are all soldiers. "Is it not touching?" said a Russian to me one day at dinner in a Petersburg restaurant, pointing at the perfect Tartar waiters. "These people under whose yoke we were are really stronger and more terrible than we are, but they are now our servants, waiters, valets. If we had become Mohammedans, the Tartars would still be greater than we. It is the Christian idea that has triumphed in us."

There stand among the deserts of Turkestan and beside the irrigated cotton fields of a new civilisation, the remains and ruins of a mediæval glory, the mosques and tombs and palaces of the days of Timour and of his loved wife, Bibi Khanum. The Russians are not touched by archæology, and have no interest in pagans, even splendid pagans. English people have considerable difficulty in obtaining permission to enter the country. So Tamerlane is little thought of. But in England, in the fifteenth and fourteenth centuries, he had a tremendous fame—you feel that fame in Marlowe's great drama:

> Holla, ye pampered jades of Asia!
> What, can ye draw but twenty miles a day,
> And have so proud a chariot at your heels
> And such a coachman as great Tamerlane?

Shakespeare burlesqued this through the mouth of Pistol:

> Shall packhorses
> And hollow pamper'd jades of Asia,
> Which cannot go but thirty miles a day,
> Compare with Cæsars, and with Cannibals,
> And Trojan Greeks? nay, rather damn them with
> King Cerberus.

England's opinion was the same as Pistol's, and the grandeur of Tamerlane was forgotten. Yet in two successive years he conquered India and Eastern Russia. He wore what was traditionally held to be the armour of King David. And, to-day, who so poor as to do him reverence? Only the beautiful name of Timour and the ruins of his tombs and mosques remain, giving a strange atmosphere of mystery and melancholy to the youngest of Russian colonies.

It is possible now to linger in the romantic idea

of all the splendour that has passed away, and to feel a strange beauty in Samarkand. I remember reading some years ago a beautiful prose poem in modern "impressionist" style, written by Zoe Pavlovska, who is, I suppose, a Russian—perhaps a Cossack. It was the story of pilgrimage to the tomb of Tamerlane's most loved princess:

I shall go to the tomb of the Emperor's daughter. It will be night, but a night when the moon is full; its clear light will guide me through the mazes of the streets of the city. These will be narrow. At dark corners I shall be afraid—muffled forms will glide past me in the deep shadows of the walls.

Now and then a light will shine from some open window. I shall stop and hear the chanting of poems, and will wait to listen, swaying in time with the rhythm.

I shall hear——

"Who will converse with me now that the yellow camels are gone? There is no friend for the stranger, save the stranger."

Then I shall creep out of the town by a turquoise-tiled gate. There they will ask me, "Where do you go?" I shall answer, showing them my box of jade, "I go to the tomb of Bibi Khanum, to lay this at her feet." I will then show them the flower in my box.

When I have reached the place I shall stand below the broken arches, and will see that they are bluer than the blue night-sky beyond them; the moon will make strange shadows. It will seem as if giant warriors are guarding her. Coming to the place where her body lies I shall say, "O beloved of Timour"—he who sleeps under a deep green sea of jade—"I have brought for you a flower." Then, though in a cloudless sky, the moon will slowly hide herself, the purple shadows will lengthen till all is black save where she lies; there each jewel on her tomb will glow into its own colour, as if lighted from within, and by this faint light I shall see the pale hands and faces of four Tartar warriors who will lift the stone which covers her. As they put it on the ground they will once more become one with the darkness.

"Brothers, I am afraid; stay near me." Thus shall I cry to them. There will be no answer, only a silence made more desolate by the continuous throbbing round of a distant drum. Slowly from the mingled light of the jewels a form will rise in garments of the colour of ripe pomegranates worked with flowers in gold; some apple-green ribbons will fall from her shoulder, and under her breasts will be a sash of vivid crimson. She will wear on her head a crown of jewels and flowers and dull gold leaves; jade and amethyst drops will fall from this crown on either side of her face, which will be painted tulip-pink and her lips scarlet; her eyes will be rimmed with black jewels ground into powder.

Then, gazing at her, I shall lay at her feet the flower from my garden, and, smiling, she will give me an amber poppy. She will say, looking into my eyes, "You ask for sleep—I would give my eternity of slumber for one moment of that sorrow I called life."

The Great War of to-day makes the past more melancholy, and, as the centuries roll out with ever newer sorrows and calamities and strifes, the faces in history seem paler, sadder. The twilight of oblivion deepens. The history of man becomes more melancholy.

VI

TO TASHKENT

THE country east of Samarkand is much greener than the country west of it. It was interesting to note that the farther east I went from the shores of the Caspian the less did the desert predominate. There was abundant life on the plains; many horses grazing, many camels carrying grey marble for the building of new palaces, many sheep. At the railway stations were Sarts, Kirghiz, Afghans, occasional Hindus, Jews—not Russian Jews, but polygamous Eastern Jews, a rich, secluded, conservative tribe, who will not own their Russian brethren or sit down with them at meat—at least, so a Jew in the train informed me.

Samarkand is outside the protectorate of Bokhara, and takes its stand now as a city of the Russian Empire. It is also a great Mohammedan centre, as much by tradition and history as by present fact; but it is now completely under Russian influence, and the future which it has is one which will show itself more and more purely Russian. Already there are 25,000 Russians there. The city is divided by one long boulevard into two parts, native and Russian, and it may be surmised that the present state of Samarkand foreshadows the future state of Bokhara, and that those three or four houses which form the Russian part of Bokhara will at length find themselves the centre of a great Russian city, standing face to face with the Eastern and ancient town. What a history has Samarkand, both in legend and in history! It was founded by a fabulous person in 4000 B.C., but only emerged into history as a place conquered by Alexander of Macedon. It was successively conquered by the various monarchs of the Huns and the Tartars and by proselytising Arabs and by the Uzbeks, and at last by the Russians in 1868. Its whole history is one of being conquered. Its people to-day are the most gentle in the world, wear no weapons, commit no violence, never even seem to get angry—I refer, of course, to the native Sarts.

A fine chain of cities—Askhabad, Merv, Bokhara, Samarkand, Tashkent—and strange to realise them to be all on the railway and in direct economic communication with Europe; it is possible to take a train from Petersburg to Tashkent, or to Bokhara, or to the Persian frontier without change. During the week in which I was at Bokhara and Samarkand work was begun on the new railway which is to run from Tashkent to Kuldzha, in Chinese Tartary, and in a little while, perhaps, we may see an agreement made and work begun in the construction of the railway to India through Persia. Russia, stopped in the Far East by the emergence of modern Japan, and thwarted in the Balkans, seemed in the time just before the Great War to be concentrating her attention on what may be called the Middle East. How open Europe

FINE-LOOKING SARTS IN OLD TASHKENT

is becoming to the East, and how easy of access is the East becoming to us! The friendship of English and Russians in Central Asia must mean a larger, stronger life for both Empires. And the development of Asia can mean much to the home Russians; they, as we, are inclined to take their own land and their capital cities as the only places of interest in the world. Already, reading some of the Moscow and Petersburg newspapers, you may alter Kipling's phrase and ask: "What do they know of Russia who only Moscow know?"

Tashkent is the capital of Russian Central Asia, and is a well-built city extending over an enormous area. It occupies a space something like a fifth of that which London occupies. There is no crowding anywhere. The houses, for fear of earthquakes, have in no case more than two storeys, and seldom that. There are many public gardens, where you may sit at white-spread tables and drink *narzan* or koumis in the dense shade of thickly foliaged trees. Tashkent is a city on an oasis. It has wonderful vegetation. Along all the streets run brisk streams of fresh water, conducted on the irrigation system from the river. There is a noise all day and all night of running water, so that if you wake in the hush of night and listen to it, you may imagine for a moment that you are living in a village among hills aleak with thousands of cascades and rivulets. How useful is this water supply to Tashkent! There is no need for water-carts; strong natives are employed with buckets to scoop water from the streams and fling it across the cobbles all day. So effectual is their work that there is never a whiff of dust, and, indeed, it is occasionally necessary to wear galoshes, the streets having been made so muddy. The streams freshen the air, keep down the dust, give life to the lofty poplars of the many avenues, and they are the convenient element for thousands of Mohammedans to wash in before saying their prayers. The streams make the town into the country. As you walk down the pavemented High Street, and look in at the truly fine shops of Tashkent, your attention may still be diverted by the dainty water wagtail that is nesting near by, and as you wait for the electric tram you observe the small heath butterfly flitting along, as much at home as upon the mountains. At night, whilst all the Russians, in white clothes, parade up and down and gossip, and the moon looks down from above the gigantic trees of the gardens and the main streets, the streams still take attention, for there proceeds from them a tumultuous, everlasting, raging chorus of frog-calling.

Up the many long streets from the old town to the new come strings of gentle-looking camels—low-backed, single-humped, long-necked camels, with sometimes as many as twenty necklaces of blue beads from below their ears. The horses, too, are much adorned with carpet cloths and coloured strings that keep the flies away. The high-wheeled carts of Bokhara have become too common in Tashkent to attract attention. Altogether, indeed, the Orient strikes one less romantically here than in Bokhara. The native population of 200,000 is very dirty and disorderly; the

OUTSIDE A GERMAN SHOP IN OLD TASHKENT

women, behind their veils, not nearly so strict or so careful; the houses not so well kept—all in dirt and ruin. On the roofs of the mosques are thousands of red poppies in bloom, and occasionally the crane's nest is to be seen on the tops of the towers whence the muezzin calls to prayer. There are booths of coppersmiths and carpet-makers and silk-workers, and caravanserai where all manner of picturesque Moslems are to be seen lying on divans and carpets or squatting over basins of tea; but all is second-hand and down-at-heel after Bokhara. With the coming of the Russians the angel of death has breathed on all that was once the grandeur of the Orient at Tashkent. Once there were no Russians in the land, and then what is now old Tashkent was the only Tashkent; it was a great Moslem city that could be pointed to geographically as such. But as the fine Russian streets were laid down, and the large shops opened, and the cathedrals were built, and the gardens laid out, the old uphill-and-down-dale labyrinth of the Eastern city slowly changed to a curiosity and an anachronism. It faded before the eyes. The next year the Russians were to celebrate the fiftieth anniversary of the conquest of the town—only the fiftieth! Poor old Tashkent, slipping into the sere and yellow leaf, passing away even as one looked, always decreasing whilst the new town is always increasing—there is much pathos in its destiny.

The natives are mostly Sarts, an absolutely unambitious people, honest, quiet, sober. Scarcely any crime ever takes place among them. A week in the year they are said to go off on a spree and get rid of the sin in them. For the rest of the time they are like lambs. They are uninterested in everything except small deals in the wares they make or sell. Their wives have rings in their nostrils for adornment—so I observed when the sun shone brightly on their black veils. A strange sight the electric tram which goes from the old town to the new and back again—crowded with men in white turbans and long robes and with Eastern women in their veils.

The foundation of the society of new Tashkent is laid by the regiments quartered there, and the fine shops exist chiefly for the custom of officers and their wives. A Grand Duke, who was banished for giving a Crown jewel to a favourite lady, lives here in exile, but he is an aged man now and receives few guests. High official personages constantly visit the colony, and consequently stay at Tashkent. The whole atmosphere is military, and there is an unusual smartness everywhere. Especially do you notice how well dressed the women are at the theatres and in the gardens, and the men accompanying them nearly all wear the sword. The middle-class Russian is out of sight, and the peasant labourer is rare, owing to the fact that the Sarts work at 9d. a day, but the Russian at 1s. or 1s. 3d. There is, however, a dandy Armenian element; young hawkers and shoeblacks and barbers who appear in the evening in white collars and cheap serges, with combed locks under felt hats, with canes in their hands.

Tashkent has now many schools, from the import-

TASHKENT. A FOOTBALL MATCH AT THE COLLEGE

ant Corpus, the military college where officers' sons are educated, to the little native school where the Russian schoolmaster tries to give Russian to the Sart. I visited the splendid military school, and was only sorry to be too late in the season to see an hour of Russian football, the game being very popular with the boys. Most of the professors at this school are officers, and I met a charming staff-captain who had known several English correspondents during the war in Manchuria. The teacher of French gave me some interesting photographs.

There are six cinema shows at Tashkent, two theatres, an open-air theatre, a skating rink, and many small diversions. The native turns up in the cinema, and there are generally long lines of turbaned figures in the front of the theatre. At the real theatres it is necessarily those who know Russian who take the seats. At the open-air theatre they play *The Taming of the Shrew*, at the Coliseum the *Doll's House* and Artsibasheff's *Jealousy*. The town has two newspapers, and on the day on which I arrived I found that the leading article of the *Courier of Turkestan* was entitled "The State of Affairs in Ulster." All Europe seemed to have its eyes on our politics, and Europe extends now as far east as Tashkent, though it is of "Central Asia" that that city claims to be the capital.

A wonderful place Tashkent. Cherries ripen there by the 1st of May, strawberries are seven copecks a pound in mid-May. Everything ripens three weeks earlier than in Russia proper. It is a fresh, fragrant city—an interesting curiosity among the cities of the world. The Russians have in it a city worth possessing. It must be said they have done their best to possess it, not merely in the letter of the law, but by improving it and governing it and giving it a Russian atmosphere. Despite camels and mosques, and natives in their turbans, and the sad call of the muezzin, you feel all the time as you go up and down the streets of Tashkent that you are in Russia.

The Kaufmann Square is, I suppose, the noblest position in the new city, all the avenues and prospects being used to frame the monument which stands there. This is the statue of General Kaufmann, who took possession of the land for the Russians. On one side of the monument is a fierce, dark, enormous, two-headed eagle in stone. But between its claws this year a dove had its nest. From behind the eagle General von Kaufmann stands and looks over his new-conquered country. On the other side of the monument there is the following inscription:

"I pray you bury me here that everyone may know that here is true Russian earth in which no Russian need be ashamed to lie."

(*From a letter of* General Kaufmann, 1878.)

Rather interesting that this should be said by a Russian with a German name.

VII

THE RUSSIAN CONQUEST

THE Russian princes, Yaroslaf Vsevolodovitch and his son, Alexander Nevsky, did homage to the Mongol khans in the thirteenth century. Timour brought back thousands of Russian slaves after his conquests, and Russia lay under the yoke of the Tartars. The Empire of Asia lasted only a little while in the hands of the dynasty of Tamerlane, and the Uzbek and the Kirghiz Cossacks appeared, waging a holy war for Islam. At the present moment there are one million Uzbeks in the province of Bokhara, three hundred and fifty thousand in Khiva, and five hundred thousand spread over the rest of Russian Turkestan, and a sprinkling in Afghanistan. The Uzbeks formed three kingdoms, Bokhara, Khiva, and Kokand. The Emirs of these states are to this day Uzbeks, but are now little more than Russian civil servants. A dependence of Kokand was Pamir, where the Karakirghiz wandered with their flocks—people now wandering on the Thian-Shan mountains in Ferghan and Seven Rivers Land, also in parts of Sirdaria and Eastern Turkestan. The Kirghiz Cossacks came south from what is now the Akmolinsk Steppe in Siberia. This race, a sort of mongrelisation of Huns and Tartars, diffused itself over the whole desert from Lake Balkhash to the Ural. In the seventeenth century they were an organised and powerful nation, with a Khan at Tashkent; but in the succeeding century there was faction and dissension, and the nation divided off into three large hordes. The great horde went to Seven Rivers Land in the Northern Ural, the middle horde to the Steppes of Akmolinsk, and the little horde to Sir-daria and the Ural. From that day their military spirit seems to have steadily waned. To-day they are as peaceful as their herds. During the years 1846 to 1854, the Russians began to penetrate the deserts of Seven Rivers Land and take the Kirghiz over as subjects. There was very little actual fighting till the Russians came into contact with the Uzbeks of Kokand, whom, however, they fought and overthrew with considerable slaughter. Verney fell in 1854, Pishpek and Tokmak in 1862. Then the Russians turned westward, and took Aulie Ata, Chimkent, and Tashkent. In 1867 Seven Rivers Land was made into a Russian province, and the stream of Russian colonisation turned out of Siberia southward toward India.

One stream of colonists was moving southward from Siberia, another was moving eastward from the Volga. One observes the rise of the Russian power. In the sixteenth century the Russian had begun to take the upper hand, and Kazan and Astrakhan, though predominantly Tartar cities, fell to the assaults of Christian arms. In the eighteenth century the peasant colonists had already come into contact with the Kirghiz Cossacks, and boundary lines had

PLEASANT COUNTRY OUTSIDE TASHKENT

to be drawn. Orenburg fell into Russian hands in 1743, and peaceful penetration followed military success. In 1847 the great horde of the Kirghiz became Russian subjects, and all the races of Central Asia began to talk about the coming advance of the Russians and the need to fight them. The Russian war of conquest was consummated in the East. From Tashkent the Russians proceeded to make war on the Bokharese. In vain did the Emir of Bokhara demand the evacuation of Tashkent by the Russians. In 1866 the Bokharese were defeated at the battle of Irdzhar, and Khodzkent was taken by storm. After heavy fighting with Uzbeks and Turkomans and great slaughter of the Mohammedans, they approached Samarkand, which at last they occupied at the invitation of the inhabitants. In 1868 a treaty was made between the Emir of Bokhara and the Tsar, whereby Samarkand and district passed to Russia.

In 1869 a Russian army crossed the Caspian and laid siege to Krasnovodsk, and attempts were made to push across the desert along the northern frontier of Persia. The Turkomans, however, offered an heroic resistance, and it was not until 1880, when Skobelef was given charge of the task of subduing the tribes, that Russia made progress. At the beginning of December, 1880, the army of Turkestan, under Colonel Kuropatkin, made over five hundred miles progress across the flying sands and took the fortress of Dengil-Tepe. Askhabad was taken, and all the fortified points in Transcaspia. Transcaspia was made into a Russian province in 1881.

In 1884 there was a short struggle, and then the ancient city of Merv fell into Russian hands, and the English began to view the Russian progress with uneasiness. There was even such a word coined as "mervousness," and Russophobes had Merv on the brain. It must be admitted we were rather backward not to treat with the Russians and obtain definite trade treaties at that time. For we lost and Germany gained a great deal of trade which we might still have retained.

Bokhara and Khiva came under Russian protection. The Central Asian Railway was built, and Russia became the most important Power in the Moslem world of Central Asia, owning as subjects so many millions of Kirghiz, Sarts, Uzbeks, Turkomans, Tekintsi, Tartars, and being neighbours of Turks, Persians, Afghans and what not. Never was such a stretch of territory, so many new subjects, or so much trade and interest won with so little trouble. It was won almost by military processions. It must be remembered that it could not have been held, nor would Russia have any real footing there to-day, but for the peasant pioneers who followed the armies and began settling the land. And the peasants would not have remained if the Government of Russia had not helped them with loans, found them suitable plots for their villages, and irrigated the desert.

Now Turkestan and Russian Central Asia are extremely loyal, peaceful and happy Russian colonies. Rebellion was put down with such severity by the

HEARTY SHEPHERDS: ALL KIRGHIZ

Russians, the defeats were with such slaughter, that the Asiatic tribesmen learned that Russia was too powerful to be trifled with; they knew they had found their masters, and submitted absolutely. The Russians overcowed their spirits, they felt there was some magic power behind them, and that human resistance was vain. Then fear gave way to placid acceptance of mastery, and the Russians began building churches and schools and fortresses and barracks, shops, towns, villages, and no one said them nay. Trade passed into the hands of Russian merchants, and new towns sprang up beside the old ones—new Bokhara beside old Bokhara, new Tashkent beside old Tashkent, and the Moslems saw unveiled the will of God. They could not have been a very warlike people really. They are not like the Mohammedans under our rule or the Turks, though it is quite possible that if, as a result of this war, a great quantity of Armenia and Turkey fell into Russian hands, the Mohammedans there would accept their fate as destiny and settle down to live as peacefully as their fellow-believers of Russian Central Asia. These are meek. During the past winter the Germans have been endeavouring to stir up Islam to fight England, France and Russia. Germany and Turkey have found a common ground. The Arabs in Mesopotamia are fighting a holy war against us. Persia has wavered; there has been ferment in India, there might have been a rising in Afghanistan, but there has been no chance of a rising of those Mohammedans who are Russian subjects. All the aborigines of Russian

Central Asia are devoted to peace, and none have any quarrel with the Russian Empire.

Russia, of course, has considerable control over her Mohammedan subjects because of the railways. The development of the lines in Central Asia has undoubtedly been a wise Imperial measure on Russia's part, and they are the best fruits of her conquest. The construction afforded certain interesting engineering problems, though it may be remarked that Russian engineers generally succeed in building railways over plains, even over deserts, but fail when they come to mountains.

The Central Asian Railway had for its original object the pacification of the Tekintsi, and was a strategic line from the Transcaspian post of Krasnovodsk to the oasis of Kizil Arvat. It was built over the desert, and was at first regarded as of a temporary military character. It cannot now be regarded as a well-built railway, is very loose, and trains are forced to go very slowly, and it is constantly in danger of sand obstruction through storms. In the progress of the military operations against the Tekintsi, Geok-Tepe was stormed in January, 1881, and the first train went through to Kizil Arvat in December of the same year. Kizil Arvat remained the terminus until the fray with the Afghans, on March 30th, 1885, when the prolongation was undertaken seriously. In June, 1885, the Tsar decided to continue the railway towards the frontier of Afghanistan, and by December 11th, 1885, the Russian military railway gangs had taken the rails

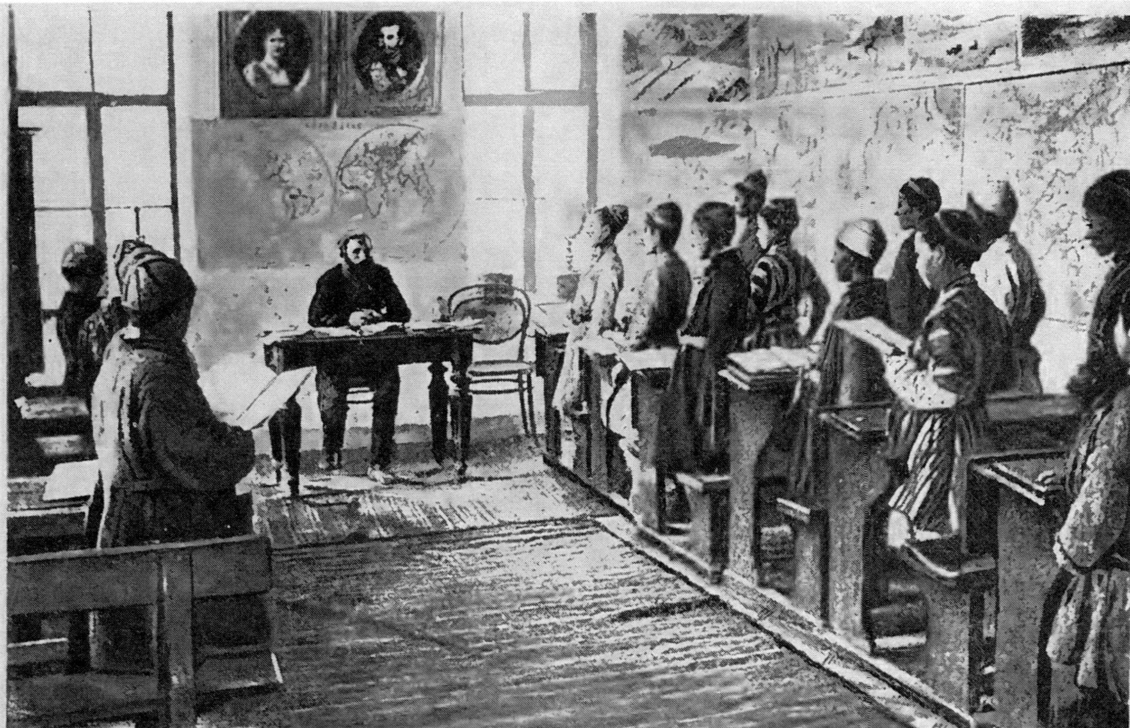

THE RUSSIAN TEACHER: A NATIVE SCHOOL IN TASHKENT

136 miles on to Askhabad, at the northern limit of Persia. Merv was annexed, the rails went on to Merv. By December, 1886, the railway had gone on to Chardzhui, on the Oxus. The red river was bridged, and the railway went on to Bokhara and Samarkand. A state service of steamers was started on the Oxus between Chardzhui and Khiva. In 1888 the completion of the line to Samarkand was celebrated, and the railway was consecrated with ecclesiastical pomp. The Russians have always given the impression that they did not intend to develop their railways, and yet they have gone on developing them all the same. They have gone south from Merv to the River Kush, on the Afghanistan frontier, and east from Khodgent to Andigan and Kokand. They have brought a main line from Petrograd, by way of Orenburg, over the deserts of Sirdaria, to the cities of Turkestan and Tashkent, and have thus a railway all the way from the Baltic to within a few hundred miles of India. In February, 1916, trains were first run on the first reach of the new railway that is to join Russia and Western China. It is now possible to go to Chimkent by train, and possibly next year to Aulie Ata. If English were in charge of this territory there would probably be more railways by now. In any case, the chief value of the railways has been the means they afforded of bloodless pacification of tribes. But their future is not so much a military future as one of trade and Imperial development.

Russia has made her Imperial conquests by force of arms, and safeguarded them by railways and colonisation. It should be remembered that before and after and all the time runs the natural stream of colonisation. The ultimate bond of unity is that which comes from the national family ties of colonisation. Nothing stands in Russia's way, and she is always quietly colonising the empty East.

An interesting yearly chart might be issued by the Russian Government showing the waves of colonisation: the new spots in forests and deserts that have been given names, the new farms, the thickening of the population in the nearer-in districts, the efflorescence of Russian enterprise at the farthest-out points whither they have gone. Several hundred Russian families are settled in Northern Persia, several hundred also in Mongolia and China. The movement goes on, and it is not primarily due to the density of population in European Russia. All Russia, excepting the few industrial regions, is under rather than over-populated. There is plenty of room. Why, then, should Russia increase? or why not? Russia has access to the empty heart of Asia. The old world is hollow at the core, and Russia has access to that great, wide hollowness, stands at the door of it and stares into the great emptiness. Then her people are wanderers; they have the wandering spirit. A cross wind blows over them, and they are gipsies—the roving heart rules the mind. They love the road and the quest. They are seekers. Even the most materialistic of them, the least religious in their outward expression, nourish dreams of success and ideas of golden climes to be found "beyond the horizon." We should eall many of them ne'er-do-wells, though as a matter of faet they are all intent to do well somewhere. They take up farms and give up farms with too little scruple, and then go farther, disgusting the official eye in one district, but knowing they will delight other official eyes farther on when they turn up with carts and cattle and belongings at some verdant, empty wilderness still farther away from the eentre of Russia.

VIII

ON THE ROAD

THERE was some difficulty in getting on from Tashkent. I had two British notes, but no bank would change them. The clerks held the paper upside down, took it to their colleagues, who were supping tea whilst they worked at their ledgers, took it to the manager to show him a curiosity, and finally returned it to me "with much regret." "Don't think we are savages," said one bank clerk, "because we do not accept your money. The fact is, we've never seen it before and cannot even read what is written on it." Another clerk, a sympathiser, advised me that there was an Englishman in Tashkent, a merchant who did much business and had an account in the bank, bade me go to him, for he would know what the notes were worth, and would no doubt accommodate a fellow-countryman. I obtained the address and sought out my compatriot. His name was something like Kellerman—not very promising. Behold one of the funniest Englishmen I ever met—as clear a German Jew as I'd ever seen in my life, scarcely speaking English, and making all the comic mistakes which Germans make with our tongue, a fat, ill-shaven, collarless old man of a greasy complexion, a middleman buying wool and horsehair and oilcakes and seed from the native Sarts and Jews and Tartars and Kirghiz. He professed to be very pleased to meet a fellow-countryman, and to be yearning for his "native land"—"a nice house in Kentish Town, all fog and wet in the streets, a nice fire, pull the blinds down, and read the '*Daily Telegraaf.*'" Every night in Tashkent he repaired to the public gardens, took a seat beside the skating rink, and watched the violent whirl of Armenian youths and their lady friends on roller-skates. Each night between ten and twelve Kellerman might be found in his place, chuckling to himself at the sight of accidents. "Causts nawthing," said he, "and it's such a pleasure to see other people break their necks or their legs."

Needless to say, he would not touch my notes; at first thought they might be false, and then offered me three pounds ten each for them. He said he wouldn't change them, but would be willing to make a deal and treat it as a matter of business. So I had to post my money to Moscow.

The next obstruction was from the police, who doubted whether I had permission to wander about in Central Asia, and it was only after I had myself looked through the books at the police-station that I found my name, almost unrecognisably spelt, in the list of those who had permission. At last I got both my money in Russian change and my *visé*, and was free to go. So I started my long journey from the limits of the railway to the frontier of China.

Through Russian Central Asia

I took train to Kabul Sai, a little station north of Tashkent, and thence set out across the grass-covered downs to Chimkent, the first point of importance on my journey. I was a little anxious lest I should be stopped by the station gendarme, for it was not to be thought that every local police authority would have my name legibly inscribed, and I did not want to be delayed waiting while Kabul Sai and a hundred other places wrote to Tashkent for information. However, I escaped attention, and, having made a good country dinner (big dinner, I should rather say) at the station buffet, I lounged about till the train went out of the station, and then, considering compass and map, I cut across country and found the road—without questions.

So I got on to my feet in Sirdaria, the land of the little horde of the Kirghiz. The plain was dusty and vast, with a great sky overhead. There were long-legged beetles that scampered through the dust of the road, tortoises and their families eating grass and dandelions, and very much taken aback when picked up and examined. Father Tortoise is big and green; his children are wee, like young crabs. There was no cultivation anywhere in sight; the first grass had already seeded and withered, but thousands of blue irises were in blossom, and the tall sheaves of their leaves contrasted strangely with the dying grass below. The sun was hot, but a fresh, travelling wind fairly lifted me as I walked. A chorus of larks overhead made the prelude to my journey.

The only people on the road were Kirghiz. Far

A KIRGHIZ GRANDMOTHER: VENDOR OF *KOUMIS*

away on the hills I noticed their great flocks of cattle and the circular tents of the nomads. There were no villages. No villages, because it was hardly "white man's country"; there was no water to drink. I thought to make myself tea, but I reckoned without my host. Where there should have been streams there was only a broken parquet of dry mud. No trees, no shade, no shelter, and, if I should find water, no fuel. The five post-wagons, drawn each by three horses and driven by enormously fat Kirghiz drivers with faces the colour of dull mahogany, went past me in a cloud of dust, and I watched them away as the sun was setting. Three-quarters of a mile away they all stopped by a wooden bridge. There was evidently water; perhaps the drivers wanted a drink. I was very joyful at the prospect of tea. When I got nearer I found that all the drivers were saying their Mohammedan prayers, and had stopped at the stream to have the conventional wash. The water was reddish-brown, with mingled mud; light could not be seen through a glass of it.

I resolved to see what could be obtained at the Kirghiz tents, put my pack down by the side of the road, and set off, with a pot in one hand and a bit of silver in the other. There were three tents on a hill, and near them many cows and goats and horses. I arrived in a whirlwind of dogs, three or four cattle dogs showing their teeth and barking and snarling as they tore round me in circles. Several women were employed tending immense pans of milk which they were boiling over bonfires made of roots. They seemed a trifle scared at first, but when I showed them the pot and pointed to the bit of silver they understood, and I was quickly put in possession of a potful of hot, smoky milk. I carried it carefully back to the place where I had slung my pack, and there I sat down, feeling rather lost or accidental, and I drank the hot milk and munched a bit of bread which I had brought from the town. The dogs followed me all the way to my resting-place, but when they saw me sit down and take things calmly they retired a distance and kept up a desultory chorus.

So I made my first meal out of doors by the roadside. The next thing was to find a place for the night. There was no variety in the country, and I could only choose a place where insects were fewer and one not over a tortoise's burrow. I had a light, home-made sleeping-sack and a plaid. The sack was made by sewing two sheets together on three sides. The sack is a useful institution; it keeps insects out and is much warmer than open clothing. I had also a mosquito net, for there are more flies here than in other parts of the world. Before making my spread I removed an elegant oak-eggar caterpillar. I am always disinclined to injure the creeping things of the earth, especially on a long journey. I feel that to a certain extent I am in their charge. This is a sort of natural superstition. Directly you kill something superfluously, horror thrills you as it thrilled the ancient mariner who shot the albatross.

I lay down in such a position as to see the sunset

RUSSIANS AND KIRGHIZ LIVING SIDE BY SIDE AT THE FOOT OF THE MOUNTAINS

in the evening and the sunrise in the morning. Sunset was stormy, but somewhere among the rose-tinged clouds a late lark sang the day out. Then stars appeared behind cloud curtains, and the night breeze carried his messages along the heath. The first breath of night was cool and pleasant, but about an hour after sunset the weather changed entirely. It became very hot and airless, and lightnings shot across all horizons. A shower of rain came down, and the stars disappeared. As I lay considering the sky I heard far off the chattering of children—chattering, laughing, and occasional bursts of singing. The sounds came nearer, and presently there emerged a troop of camels, twelve huge camels stalking out of the night, and on their backs men, women and children, tents, goods. A little family of wanderers crossing the wilderness in the night! They came so near to me that the first camel snorted as he passed, and it was necessary for me to sit up and warn the others off. I had not anticipated that there might be people travelling across country in the night. They passed, and the quietness of night resumed its sway. The clouds thickened, and lightning shimmered under them; it began to rain again, and then stopped, and the stars once more came up, and then the clouds thickened once more, and once more rain came down on me with rapid tapping. So the whole night, and it was a pleasant tempering of the heat. I slept happily, and it was a long while before I wakened.

When I reopened my eyes it was to look at the

seven stars standing over a blue-grey, vaporous cloud, and looking like some uncanny Asiatic frying-pan over a fire. There was scarcely a star but for them, and south and east and west were all dark. It did not occur to me that it was near dawn. But suddenly a voice of liquid melody burst from the sky, and after it, as at a signal, a whole chorus of larks sang together away high up in the rain-wet vault of the sky.

I slept an hour longer, and it was morning. For my breakfast I visited another Kirghiz tent, and this time obtained a pot of mare's milk. A dwarf-like old woman was squatting on a carpet in the middle of the tent, and when I said "koumis" she at once got up and brought me a tall wooden jar. I held my pot, she tipped up the jar, and poured out the koumis. Good that Kirghiz women are not so strictly hidden as other Mohammedans of their sex!

About ten o'clock I fell in with two soldiers walking to Verney (some six hundred miles), their guns and knapsacks having gone before by wagon. They reckoned they would be more than a month on the road. No doubt they would march the journey in better style with a whole column, but as it was they were inclined to stop every two hundred yards and take off their boots; one wore jackboots, and rags for stockings, and the other Kirghiz sandals tied with string over bare feet. He told me light shoes were better than heavy boots, but I knew better.

"Heavy going?" said I.

"Yes, heavy. No water, and no one understands us in the Kirghiz tents."

We shared what remained of my koumis.

"Where do you come from?"

"Voronezh fort. And you?"

"From England."

"Have you served in the army?"

"No. We don't need to unless we want to, you know; our soldiers receive wages."

"How much?"

"Fifty copecks a day," said I, "and a premium when they retire."

"And they only give us seventy copecks a month. There's a difference! How long do you have to serve? Ah! We have only three years to serve. But I've seen your soldiers," said the Russian.

"Where?"

"At Teheran. We stood side by side with them there. But afterwards it was found we were not necessary, and they moved us back."

One of the soldiers was inclined to talk, the other not. Suddenly the silent one asked: "What are you doing here—making plans?"

"No," said I apprehensively; "I'm just walking along through the country to see what it is like. Afterwards I write about it."

"For a library, so to speak?"

"That's it."

After much self-questioning on the subject of where water was to be found next, we came at last to a brook where there was clear water. It was warm and salt to the taste, but I decided to make tea. The soldiers sat by and grinned incredulously. I should not have been able to light a fire, but that, like the cunning younger brother in the fairy-tale, I had been picking up every bit of wood that I chanced to see along the roadway. I had early realised how difficult it was to find fuel and how precious any stray bit of wood really was. By the stream there was nothing to burn but hay. "Now shift yourselves," said I, "and go and find some dry hay, the driest; we shall need all the fuel we can get." They obeyed like good soldiers, and the fire burned and the kettle boiled and the tea was made. What tea! No one would have touched it in Tashkent, but out here on the road we drank it to the last drop and left the tea-leaves parched.

The soldiers then stretched themselves out to sleep, and I went on. A mile on I met a Kirghiz lad carrying a scythe on his back, and he rejoiced in my company and talked to me exuberantly in his native tongue. I replied to him in Russian, but as he did not understand that, but still went on talking, I reverted for amusement to English. One thing was clear—he admired my ring very much, and several times he took up my hand as we walked and looked at the ring and exclaimed.

When we got to his tent I bade him fetch me some mare's milk, and so I got my evening meal. I had never tasted koumis before this day, and had generally regarded it as more in the nature of medicine than food. I knew that Russians suffering

A TENT OF LONELY NOMADS ON A SUMMER PASTURE IN CENTRAL ASIA

from catarrh of the stomach and internal troubles were ordered by doctors to go to Kirghiz country and live exclusively on koumis. Now it seemed I had to live on it, more or less, for several weeks. Some say it is as invigorating as champagne; I do not know. It is certainly a pleasant drink and good food.

That night I slept out till ten, and then thunder and the rain forced me to pack up and search for shelter. Eventually a little old man whom I met in the dark conducted me to a Kirghiz caravanserai. *Sarai* is Russian for a shed or barn, and the caravanserai is the shed where the caravan puts in, otherwise an inn. I was accommodated on an old carpet on a dried mud floor. There were a score of men in the room. Some were snoring, some were smoking hookahs, one was playing a three-stringed guitar, and the rest were squatting round a little kerosene lamp on the floor, dealing out grimy cards, calling out numbers, gathering in copecks.

The roof of the inn was all canes and earth, and I surmised that grass was growing above it. The walls were tattered and old, and occasionally a fat scorpion wandered along them. There was a black and white duck in one corner sitting on a basket of eggs. I lay away from the walls. "Not good to sleep indoors," I reflected; "fresher and quieter on the heath; but I don't want to get soaked."

After my night in the Kirghiz caravanserai I was regaled in the morning with millet bread and tea. My host charged me 2d. for bed and breakfast, and I resumed my journey. It was over a moorland country, high and windswept. All day I was climbing uphill to view points, or plunging downhill into the rough pits that lay between them. The sun was a ghost in the haze of the sky; there was a tempering of the light, and even now and then a cloud shadow cast over the fields, and it was delicious to look at the myriads of crimson poppies set in meadows of rank grass.

I was in better country; there were more streams, more people, more cattle. There were snowy mountains on the horizon. Some freshness from the snow came from them. I sat on a sun-bathed crown of the downs and watched the lambs playing; white, brown, yellow, black lambs, very pretty to look at, very lively. And immense camel herds came stalking up to me as if released from some pen, groaning, whining, grunting, lying in the dust and rolling over, getting up again convulsively, tolling the lugubriously sounding bells that hang under their necks. There were many baby camels no bigger than donkeys; as they came along they indulged in ungainly scampering, which made it look as if their hind legs were fighting their fore legs.

Pleasant for me to sit and watch them idly! How different the feelings of a dozen prisoners whom I saw being marched along my road by two armed guards, a pitiful little troop of men, some of them stripped to the waist, because they thought it cooler so, all very dusty and limp, and all carrying in their hands blue, empty kettles which they hoped to fill at springs or streams by the way. Alas!

there was no water fit to drink anywhere along that road! Poor prisoners. What to them were poppy fields, or camel herds, or beautiful views! There was probably just one thought in each and every one's head: "When shall I get a drink?" or "When shall we come to a piece of shade?"

The prisoners went on in the dust; I remained behind in the free air. In the afternoon I saw a samovar steaming outside a mud hut, and so went up and was allowed to have tea with a Kirghiz family. Not nomads these Kirghiz, but settled inhabitants with passports or papers. The Russian Government is very anxious to get these wandering folk out of tents into immovable dwellings. There squatted down to tea the owner of the hut, in a rust-coloured cloak; his wife, in a bright yellow "cover-all"—hold-all, you might almost say; a boy, in white cotton slops; and a little dusky girl, naked to the waist, but wearing cotton trousers, having a silver chain round her neck, and her black hair in twelve long and slender plaits, each loaded at the end with a little silver weight that kept them from getting mixed up and looking untidy. The mother, in yellow, had a sort of wire puzzle in her ears for ear-rings, on her head a high, white turban. She was by no means a beauty. She looked as if originally she had been made without a mouth, and a neighbour had opened a place for it with a blunt knife. The Kirghiz women are not by any means feminine or attractive in appearance. As we squatted, each with a basin in our hands, in came a neighbour from the fields. She wore a white turban and a white gown. Her face was deep oak-stain. She had a sash of scarlet at her middle, wore jackboots, and had on her wrists three bracelets of the serviette-holder type. She was a woman cowherd, just in from the fields. In her hands she carried a little spinning stick with circular leaden weight at the bottom of it, and on to this she dexterously pulled camel hair out of one hand whilst with the other she twirled it into thread. She was evidently *persona grata* in the hut. She had the face of a pirate—a great, big, tanned, jolly, horse-like sort of face.

After tea the boy and girl ran off to the flocks, the women went on spinning, and the father brought out a bull with a ring through his nose and a chain and rope hanging from it. He put a bit of hide on the beast's back, and then, to my astonishment, mounted and rode away over the hills. I sat in a shady corner and watched the afternoon turn to evening.

Presently out of the blue sky came a hurricane shower of hail and rain, flashing through the dazzling sunshine and yet never obscuring it. It was big, stinging hail, but none of the Kirghiz seemed to mind it. I could see all the children of the village disporting themselves with the lambs and the calves on the hill opposite. Not till twilight did they return —and then there was for me one of the prettiest sights. All the children came in riding bareback on calves or sheep, and driving them forward with kicks of their little bare feet. The little dusky girl sat

SARTS SELLING BREAD: THE *LEPESHKA* STALL

astride of a golden-brown lamb, and her brother on an unwilling brown calf. Following the lamb came the anxious mother ewe, and following the calf a bellowing old black cow. Many children came up, and there was a gay gathering and a delicious noise of mirth and jollity at the end of the day. As a reward to the ewes and the lambs the children brought them millet bread and fed them from their hands. The ewes did all but speak to the children, and the way they took the millet bread from them spoke of an unusual intimacy between children and animals. The sheep were not worried or stupefied by the children's pranks; they were watchful, wilful, and almost as mischievous as the children themselves. In these wild places of the world where there is no civilisation and no pretension on the part of man to be more than an animal himself—where, moreover, man lives in the midst of great herds where all business and doing seems to be the breeding of young—the children of men and the children of the herds are much more akin. The birth of children synchronises with the birth of lambs and foals, and is associated in the aboriginal mind. One understands how the eyes of the ancient Israelites and Egyptians, those primeval shepherd and nomadic peoples, were fixed upon the process of birth. They lived also in the midst of the animal world.

At nightfall carpets were spread outside the hut for the people to sleep on. They also lived the night with the stars. But the children stayed long with the lambs, and I imagine in some cases slept with them.

I, for my part, decided to push on for Chimkent * in the cool of the evening, and I got into the little town about ten o'clock at night. Chimkent is a miniature of Tashkent, but without the great buildings and shops in the Russian half. The same wide town—when you come to it you are not there; it is necessary to go on and on. The same gullies running along every street—only the water in them is less muddy than at Tashkent. The Sartish shops again. The dazzling cinema shows once more. I made for a brilliant illumination, thinking it might be an hotel, but it was the cinema theatre "Light." Cinema theatres all have names in Russia, none more common than this one of "The Light."

I found an inn at length, and a room. Next morning I went out for provisions. Chimkent has a little reputation as a watering-place, and chiefly because of the supply of koumis! Russians are very fond of going to outlandish places in order to be "cured," and koumis is the cure of Chimkent. It is a beautiful little town, however. Chimkent has its mountain background, its white-stemmed, magnificent poplars, its old ruins, its fortifications. The Russians live more freely than usual. No passport was asked of me at the inn where I stayed. There was no Government monopoly of the sale of vodka.† There seemed to be fewer police about.

* Connected by rail with Tashkent since my tramp across the country.

† As the Government never exercised a monopoly of the sale of vodka in Russian Central Asia the Tsar's edict did not apply to these regions. However, I believe the sale of intoxicating liquor has been greatly restricted by the local authorities.

The Bazaar of Chimkent

The Sartish bazaar was full of life and colour; carpenters, smiths and metal workers doing their work at open booths; koumis merchants standing behind gallon bottles and little glasses, inviting you to sit down there and then and drink a glass, the white of the milk gleaming suggestively through the gloomy green of the bottle; silk and cotton vendors exposing marvellously gaudy wares to veiled females who tried to look at the stuff without exposing their faces, a difficult manœuvre; strawberry hawkers; hawkers of *lepeshka;* carpet vendors; saddle vendors. There were high stacks of gaily coloured wooden saddles. A Kirghiz woman, riding astride of a pony, and yet having a dusky baby at her open breast, came and bought just such a saddle.

What remains most brightly in my mind was a long row of silvery-grey wolf skins exhibited at one shop. It was almost as if the animals themselves were looking at you. It reminded me of what winter must be like in this land—not mild, as one might expect, but intensely cold as long as it lasts. The moors are full of dangers from wolves. It was hereabouts, some years ago, that a whole wedding party of thirty or forty people perished on their way from the church to the bride's house. The distance was only twenty miles, and in that time the wolves tore down all the horses and all the people except one Kirghiz driver, who by sacrificing the last-left couple, the bride and groom, and throwing them to the wolves, escaped to tell the tale and not feel shame. The Kirghiz would not feel shame at such an act—they are somehow outside codes of honour and chivalry and religion. They are not savages, but they are not civilised.

I spent a day altogether at Chimkent. Before resuming my tramp I bought myself a bottle in which to keep water or milk against a thirsty hour on the road. At the shop where I bought it a strange variety of wares was exposed; first Caucasian wine, then local wine—vodka, called here table wine—cognac, liqueurs, then ikons, flowers for your grave, matches and tobacco. Very suggestive, I thought. The landlady was rather taken aback at my remarks, and said that in a small place like Chimkent one could not have a separate shop for ikons or for flowers or for vodka, and her brother was a joiner, and she could take orders for coffins.

At Chimkent I struck colonial country, the main stretch of Russian colonisation extending eastward from Tashkent. I set out over a very worn switchback road, through irrigated fields of barley, through hayfields, where Russians were at work, past Russian farmhouses, into a country entirely different from that which I had been traversing. For the time being the Kirghiz was out of sight and I was in a Russian colonial district, a sort of Southern Siberia, full of interest and promise. At dusk I came to an encampment of fifty or sixty emigrants, with their wagons and horses. Many fires were burning, and iron pails full of soup were simmering over them; samovars were steaming, children were skirling and playing, someone was playing a concertina, and many drunkards were singing. Familiar Russian songs rent the air—the old songs which Russians never seem to abandon, and perhaps never will abandon, even when everybody knows the latest music-hall catch.

I slept the night on a hillock overlooking the road, and it was better than at the inn, even though there was a thunder-shower. The larks sang the day out again. I listened to the cuckoo calling and to the conversation of the blue crows that kept visiting me, finding out something, flying away, and then returning with brethren; watched the stars and the clouds, and slept.

I had now struck the main road from Tashkent to the Chinese frontier, and the prospect of my journey changed from one of solitary wandering over sandy wastes to one full of life and interest in the company of Russian colonists and Oriental traffickers. From the moment I wakened up on the hill-side on my first morning after leaving Chimkent, I was not out of the hearing of songs and laughter and chattering, nor out of the sight of wagons, carts, camel trains and people.

The road was really four roads, each separated by streaks of trampled grass-grown mud, now dried or drying after many thunder-showers. On the southern side you are accompanied by snowy mountains for hundreds of miles. You would think that you could walk to them in half an hour and get a handful of snow, so clear is the atmosphere that shows them, but they are at least twenty miles distant. They are, first, the Alai Tau, and then the Alexandrovsky Mountains, and then what is known as the Trans-Ilian Alai Tau, and many of their peaks are over ten thousand feet high, but are not named and little known. On the north side of the road stretches the desert in spring, now green to the horizon, but already turning yellow here and there under the blaze of the sun. On either hand one sees far away clusters of grey tents of the Kirghiz, and near them their herds of cattle—black patches that are horses, red patches that are cows, grey, white and brown masses like many maggots, and they are sheep. There are also many camels far away on the hills, looking like little twists of thick rope with knots in the middle.

Nearly all the traffic at this season is going eastward, and each morning, when the horses are put in and the wagoners make up the caravan once more, it is with eyes and faces toward the dawn.

The emigrant caravan starts an hour before sunrise; the camp breaks up and the oxen and horses are put to, and the long day of creaking and blundering and toiling onward commences. I was regularly wakened up by the road which had wakened before me, the moving caravans and the traders' carts.

> The stars are setting and the caravan
> Starts for the dawn of nothing. Oh! make haste!

I generally slept at a distance of about a hundred yards from the actual highway, in order to avoid being run over at night. Even so, I was frequently in some danger of being trodden on before dawn, and at least sure to be wakened early by the traffic on the road. Upon occasion there were whole hordes and patriarchal families on the roads, with their camels and sheep and horses, their white-turbaned women riding on bulls, and pretty girl-brides on caparisoned palfreys.

We journeyed from village to village, and each was an artificial oasis made by the Russian colonists and irrigation engineers. Every ten, fifteen or twenty miles there was a substantial Russian village; the farther I went the more distance there was between these settlements, but still the actual chain was kept up unbroken to the far east of the colony, and the maps which we have of these deserts are unrepresentative in that they show blank spaces with a scattering of Tartar names of places. The map should now be well marked with Russian names. Each village is a shady shelter, alive with the running water of the irrigation canals, wherein are trailing families of ducks. There are long lines of splendid poplar trees, solid houses, schools, shops, a church, post office, municipal buildings, and so on. A notice-board tells the number of souls and the date of the foundation of the village.

When the long caravans of new colonists came to a settlement they tied their horses and oxen to trees, repaired to inns, sought out people who had come from their part of Russia, and made merry with them. The village was a great sight when one of the long caravans had come in.

A little respite from the hot road, and then on once more. I see a Kirghiz riding with reins in one hand and a hawk in the other. The Kirghiz are great hawkers, using different hawks for different game. I meet a Sartish cart in which are five soldiers coming home from Verney, where they have received their discharge—several hundred miles from a railway station—and they have hired a native cart, and are asleep in the bottom of it. At last I come to a tumbling mountain stream, and it is good to have a swim and make myself tea in the shadow of the great bridge which takes the high road across the water. When a great band of colonists arrives here, there is an astonishing scene of peasant men and women bathing. They take to the water as if their very bodies were thirsty.

We pass through Mankent, one of the few native towns remaining, and that tending to be swallowed up by Russia also; and there, at a Sartish shop, stay for koumis—very bad koumis compared with what the Kirghiz gave me in their tents. Coming out of Mankent I fell in with a band of rich emigrants going from Stavropol, in South Russia, to beyond Kopal. They had twenty-four ox-drawn carts and twelve drawn by horses, and in the carts were their household goods—tables, chairs, beds and bedding—agricultural implements, reaping and binding machines, ploughs, grindstones, saws, axes, even metal baths, barrels, guns, pots and what not in such miscellaneity and promiscuity, mixed with mothers and babies, that it was touching to see. The oxen, in their wooden yokes, were fine beasts, and the emigrants tended them on foot. Every wagon was accompanied by one or two on foot, who flicked off the flies and encouraged the oxen along, sang songs, and shouted to one another. Every wagon had buckets swinging at the side. One wagon had several cages of doves fixed on to it; to another a poor old dog was tied, and came along unwillingly. In short, everything they could bring from Mother Russia to the new land the emigrants had brought.

I accompanied them up on to a wild moorland, on to a great plateau, where we spent the night after passing out of Mankent.

As I tramped thus across Russian Central Asia the great event that should change everything was hidden behind the screens of the future. The gentle and innocent present was more interesting than past or future. It is touching to go over my diary and see how guilelessly and unsuspectingly I and everyone was walking the time road that led so soon—if we only could have known it—to the precipice of war. The every-day was friendly, even though it contained storm or adventure or privation. We were familiar with mornings and evenings as with long known and trusted friends. As we look back at them they have a sinister aspect as of police conducting us by stages to some frontier. It is with these feelings that I look back now to my long tramp to the mysterious city of Aulie Ata, a famous shrine in the days of Tamerlane. Each night I slept under the stars, each day journeyed pleasantly forward under a tropical sun.

One night, near the new Russian village of Antonovka, there was an appalling sunset—through a barrel-shaped thundercloud into a sea of fire; and directly the sun went below the horizon the lightning became visible in the cloud, and I watched it running through the dark veils of vapour in ropes and loops and flying lassoes of silver. The thunder rolled lugubriously, and far away I could see the rain pouring in continuous flood, the black fringe of the cloud torn from heaven down to earth. I wondered had I not better pack up and go down to the village. But a little wisp of clear sky, containing one pale star, expanded itself slowly and drove away the great lightning-riven barrel and banished every cloud, and it was clear and the thunder was not, and the night was dry and starry. Dawn next morning was clear and cold, and at the sound of cart-wheels on the highway below me I gladly took the road again—quick march to get warm. In an hour, however, the sun was already too ardent a friend, and I took shelter in a caravanserai, a cubical mud hut with neither chair nor table, and from the samovar steaming on the floor I prepared my morning tea—put some tea from a packet in my knapsack into my pot, and then filled up with boiling water from the samovar. The village street outside was full of life, crowded with wagons and wagoners standing half in the bright new light of day and half in the deep, damp shadow of mud walls and banks. I sat down opposite the village school. The school door was wide open, and I saw all the village children sitting in desks round the mud-built room. There were about thirty children, and they were a pretty sight, the boys in turkey-red cotton trousers, the girls in red frocks, with their black hair in plaits. There was only one row of desks, but it went right round the room. In the middle space were two teachers squatting on a carpet spread on the floor. Each and every child was saying his lessons at the top of his voice, and sing-song—but not the same thing, all different, according to the page the boy or girl was at, some far behind, another far in front. These were all Sart children.

I walked all day after this with a damp towel hanging from under my hat, and as fast as the towel dried I made it wet again from my water-bottle. Everyone on the road was thirsty and hungry, and I said to myself: "The next village is called Cornucula; let's hope it will turn out to be Cornucopia!" And it was indeed a horn of plenty, and I shared there a roast chicken and a pitcher of milk with a companion of the road, a poor old horseman who had a horse but who had no money, and was begging his way home to Aulie Ata.

"How much did you give for your horse?" said I.

"It cost thirty-five roubles originally, with saddle and bridle and bags. I don't know what it's worth now. It's peaceful, that's the main thing, and it lives on grass."

This is really the country where wishes are horses, for you see beggars riding. What a lot of wishes astray on these mountains!

"Where have you been?" I asked.

"Looking for a job."

"Where?"

"On the new railway."

"Couldn't you get one?"

"No; there were thousands waiting, and they only took on two hundred, and these at the lowest wage piece-work." He mentioned some figure the cubic foot.

"How much can a man earn in a month if he goes at it hard?" I asked.

"Twenty roubles (two guineas), not more," said my acquaintance.

Imagine it—for a job of ten shillings a week, bestial labour, in the desert, under the Central Asian sun, something like a twenty to one excess of supply over demand of labour, and the people waiting weeks, months, on the chance. Surely nowhere but in Russia could such a phenomenon be noted. There, as nowhere else in the world, is a tremendous superfluity of white men's hands. A firm of contractors has this job from the Government; according to their schedule, labour was to be paid for at a certain rate —a very low rate—but, seeing the expectancy and the sad plight of the mobs of unemployed waiting at the starting-point of the new line, they quite cheerfully make a handsome reduction in favour of themselves.

The Asian Night

After our meal the beggar horseman went off on his nag, and I wandered through the village on foot. Among other establishments in the village was a photographer's, and outside his little house was a notice:

> THOSE WISHING TO HAVE THEIR PHOTOGRAPHS TAKEN MAY HAVE A SHAVE FREE

I went in to the photographer, and saw many photographs of shaven colonists, all very stiff and serious looking. These were chiefly pioneers and passers-by, the people of the caravans. It is strange how unhappy everyone looks in a provincial portrait. The photographer, however, did a good business.

I settled down for the evening and the night in the sight of lovely mountains. The sky cleared of wisps of cloud and discovered the stars. The new moon, born surely that day, was but a hair of silver in the west, and sank an hour after sunset, followed by a beautiful attendant star. As I lay on the heath and looked upward, the first constellation just formed, and it was the seven stars, delicate and lovely in the half-night, as dainty as a maiden's ornament. Showers of meteors, half observed, slipped out of the dark into the dark; long single meteors left, as it were, phosphorescent trails of light behind them. The Asiatic mountains drew their cloaks round them, hardened their faces, and slept as they stood away in the background. It became a night of countless stars, each star a jewel set in the darkness. The night wind came waving over the grass, full of health, gentleness and warmth. It was never still all night, but never cold, and never a cloud touched the vast glittering sky.

Next night before falling asleep I witnessed an unusual phenomenon. Away in the north a strange black ribbon seemed to be let down from a cloud, and it fluttered in the air. I thought of America and advertisement devices and of aeroplanes all in a second, and then remembered I was in Central Asia, far away from the inventions of civilisation. The ribbon came nearer, and as it passed overhead took a wedge-shaped formation, and I saw it was composed entirely of birds. They were flying across the heaven at a breathless speed, now in the clouds, now out, and never breaking up their ranks, the big birds seeming to be thick on top of one another in the front. On approaching the line of snow peaks in the south, they defiled into a long, single line, looking like some aerial train, and then easily, rapidly, passed over Talas Tau and Hindu Kush to India, as I surmised, just four hundred miles as they fly. The moon that night was a crescent of pearl, and stayed a little longer in the sky. I watched her night by night till she was full grown, and rose in the east the time the sun was setting, and reigned in the sky the whole night. How pleasant and serene the night weather remained! All night long the breeze rippled and flapped in my sleeping-sack and crooned in the neck of my water-bottle. Far up on the hills lights twinkled in Kirghiz tents, and in the illumination of moonlight I faintly discerned black masses of cattle beside which boys watched all night, playing their wooden pipes and singing their native songs to one another.

As far as High Village (Visokoe) the road remains with the Russians, and their villages abound. After Visokoe there is forty miles of moorland to Grosnoe, and then for a hundred miles there is not a Russian settlement except the town of Aulie Ata. Journeying became very difficult when the road was over deserted, empty moorland. The sun poured down, there was not a glimpse of shade anywhere, seldom any water, and seldom anything to eat. Even the grass was disappearing, and the Kirghiz everywhere were moving, following the spring, with their tents and their cattle and their camels, away from the scorched plains up to the fresher slopes of the mountains. Often I rigged up my plaid as a tent, often sat in the pale grey shadow of an ancient ruin or a tomb. The emigrants who tended the oxen on the road were fain to climb into the canvas-covered wagons and sleep, leaving the slow cattle to trudge with the extra load through the dust. Russian Ascension Day came, and the road was perfectly empty—for no one would travel on a festival. All day long I met but one man, a native on a camel. For a long time we walked within sight of one another, he allowing the camel to graze when it felt inclined, but every now and then giving it a kick, to which it responded by a plaintive groan and a jangling of the bell round its neck.

One might ask where is Tamerlane, where the

warriors, the robbers, the camp followers of the hordes? The Easterns you meet are all gentle as children. No one needs to carry a weapon. Where is the old spirit of fighting? The answer might be found, I suppose, in the thousands of Cossacks and Russians who, later in the same year, returned along these roads to fight against the Germans.

The day before reaching Aulie Ata, in the heat of noon, I came in sight of a green patch on the moors, and sought and found a bubbling spring of clear water. "Here is the place," thought I, "to make my long-deferred cup of tea," and I cast my knapsack on the moor and looked around for a spot on which to make a fire. I had gathered a few sticks along the road in case of need, so I had the foundation of a little blaze. With what trouble did I keep that fire going till the kettle boiled, rushing about for wisps of withered weed, hunting for roots, for a straw, for anything that would burn, and all the time anxious lest in my absence the pot should capsize. At last, as I stood over the fire, there were symptoms of boiling, and I was just rejoicing. Then suddenly all grew black around me, and I lost control of my body and fell down. Such was the effect of the burning sun on my neck and head. Perhaps this was something in the nature of a sunstroke. Be that as it may, even at the moment of falling I got up again. For what was my vexation to realise, even at the moment that I fell, that my kettle had capsized. The fact brought me to my senses. I hardly touched the ground before I started up again to save the water and the fire. No luck; the water was all spilt, the fire out, and the kettle lying in the ashes. I did not trouble to pick the kettle up. I sat down by the spring, soaked a handkerchief, put it on my head, took out my mug, and drank water—such a lot of water.

What a day! I was to feel the effects of my sunstroke. A great thirst took possession of me, and when I got to Aulie Ata a touch of fever, which I had to fight.

Aulie Ata the ancient, the tomb of the Holy One, is a mysterious and umbrageous city. I became aware of its trees on my outward horizon early one afternoon, when the mighty sun had just passed the zenith and was beginning to beat on my shoulders. I had made my siesta at noon in a tent I contrived with my plaid. I tied one corner to a telegraph pole and tied stones to the other corners, and somehow made a canopy, and I lay in a blaze of diffused light on the hard, dry, sandy steppe. Though the wind blew, it was burning hot, and my right hand was swollen and smarting, for I hold a strap of my knapsack with it as I march. I drank the last drain of water in my water-bottle and made the melancholy reflection that Central Asia is not a land to tramp in. I heard the jun-jun-jun of camels, but did not care to put out my head to look at them. I wished I had a tent, or a stout and voluminous umbrella.

Still, one couldn't stay in this spot all day, so I untied my blanket from the telegraph pole and the stones, packed my knapsack, and set off again into the dazzling brilliance of the open country. In about half an hour I espied an old ruin in the wilderness, and ran along to it, and found at the foot of the blanched wall three feet of intense shadow, in which it was just possible to sit and keep in. A villainous-looking scorpion seemed to be of the same opinion as I was, but I was too lazy to kill him, so I just flicked him off into the sun. Oh for some water, or some milk, or some koumis, but not a Kirghiz tent was to be seen all around. The Kirghiz were twenty miles away up in the green valleys of the Alexander mountains, where was pasture for their herds.

On the road once more! And then like a mirage I saw the long dark streak of Aulie Ata on the eastern horizon. It was twelve to fifteen miles away, but I thought it to be quite near. So clear is the atmosphere, so prominent in the wide emptiness of the desert are the trees of the Russian settlements, that one is constantly deceived as to the distance of the place in front of one. And I greatly rejoiced when I saw Aulie Ata; and although I was tired I resolved to get there without further resting by the way. I walked and walked and my shadow grew longer as the sun went down in the west behind me; but still the line of trees seemed as remote as ever. Several times I asked myself: "Am I not nearer?" and I was obliged to confess that I seemed no nearer. It was like walking towards the horizon. "There is something of magic about this city," I thought.

It was long before I came even to the irrigated

fields of the settlers, and only late in the dusk I arrived at the first outlying streets of the town, and went in with the procession of cows returning from the steppe to be milked in the yards of the colonists. In the midst of the clamour and dust I arrived. As I hadn't had anything to drink since noon, and I daren't touch the water of the irrigation canals, I was just about as thirsty as it is possible to be. I determined to stop at the first caravanserai, and there I had a big teapot and five or six little basins of tea and a bottle of koumis, and I stopped at the next caravanserai and had a bottle of lemonade and seltzer water. Tired as I was, however, I did not seek a night's lodging, but went first to the post office, about two miles from the entrance to the town, and I obtained the telegram I knew would be waiting for me from Russia. I had arranged a little code so that certain things I wanted to know could easily be told me "by wire." Letters take weeks. It had been pleasant to look at the wires by the roadway as I walked and reflect that a message to me was, perhaps, winging its way past me. And, sure enough, at the little post office my telegram was waiting.

After the post office I found a place at which to stay, a Russian inn called the Hotel London; and so, to justify its name, took a room in it and felt glad to have reached a city, even Aulie Ata the ancient.

Aulie Ata is a strange town hid behind the foliage of its long lines of trees. The running water courses along the canals, and, as at Chimkent and Tashkent, bull-frogs croak in chorus. The foundation of the settlement is Mohammedan. It was once a great holy place of the Moslems, the shrine of some antique teacher. But Russia has taken the upper hand and given a different aspect. There are scores of mosques lifting their slender minarets above the verdure of the trees, but most of the houses are Russian houses. And there are hotels, cinema-shows, restaurants, theatres, as well as farmhouses, shops, *sarais*, mud dwellings, and fixed Kirghiz tents.

Darkness had long since settled down on the town when I went forth to find a restaurant. Here every restaurant is a *sad*, or garden. It is fenced with bamboo; the tables are set among flower-beds and gravel paths, and there is trellis-work with festoons of greenery hanging from it, strange light and shade betwixt the moonlight and the lamplight and the darkness.

I found a garden kept by an Armenian, and had dinner by myself at a table under a fruit-laden cherry tree luridly illumined and yet only partially illumined by the blaze of a huge spirit lamp. Moths whirred into vision and descended towards the white table-cloth, and heavy beetles and locusts stunned themselves against the spirit lamp, and all manner of winged vermin and midget danced in the light which seemed to hang like drapery from the tree.

A waiter had taken my order, and a cook far away was cooking what I had ordered, and I sat and rested and considered the day which at noon had

THE NATIVE ORCHESTRA: SEE THE MEN WITH THE TEN-FOOT HORNS, "TRUMPETS OF JERICHO" AS THE RUSSIANS CALL THEM

been ablaze in my improvised tent on the steppe and at night was here in a lighted but shadowy restaurant-garden in a city.

My dinner was brought, and all the time I was eating my *shashleek* (bits of lamb roasted on a skewer over charcoal) I listened to an unearthly hubbub of bands—or of fire hooters, I could not tell which. Every ten minutes there was an awesome silence, and then there outbroke the blast of a horn, three times repeated, that sounded like the trump of doom, *terumm, terumm, terumm;* then came the sound of bagpipes and a throbbing of many drums, the horns breaking through the lesser music at intervals and lifting the roof of the sky. This was an appalling accompaniment to my meal. I had never heard anything like the sound of that horn:

Terum—m—m,
Terum—m—m,
Terum—m—m.

It was like the blast

Of that dread horn,
On Fontarabian echoes borne,
Which to King Charles did come,
When Roland brave and Olivier,
And every paladin and peer,
On Roncesvalles died!

Like the horn of Roland blown in the desert and heard three hundred leagues away. After dinner, I went off to find by ear the origin of this hubbub. I went along towards the sound, and found it proceeded from a native orchestra standing on the roof of a circus building. Here two tall Sarts held in their hands horns ten feet long. They lifted these horns to the sky and balanced them on their lips; they lowered them and blasted their music over the roofs of the houses of the city; they presented them at the heads of the crowd of sightseers, and made many put their fingers to their ears and walk away: it was a terrifying and astonishing noise. It was wonderful, however, the effect of the three angles at which the horns were blown. You felt the first one went right over the town, it was a voice from the stars, it leapt from the dark emptiness of the desert on one side to the dark emptiness of the desert on the other side of the city; the second, blown at the people's heads, was in the town and at the town, and caused the houses to tremble; the third was blown, as it were, to the dead.

These horns are traditional instruments of the Sarts, though it is said there are only a few men alive who can blow them. It needs great strength, and the degenerating race does not produce such fine men as it did. The Russians call them the "trumpets of Jericho."

An astonishing advertisement for a circus. The sound of these horns was too much for my temperament, and I fought shy of the show, though I should otherwise have liked to go in. Still, a new stage in my journeying had been reached, and I sought diversion, found a theatre, and bought a seat to see a romance of ideal love. There were seven people in the theatre, and after an hour we were all given our money back and told that the company had gone to see the circus. I then went to the cinema to see the much-advertised "spectacle" of "A Prisoner of the Caucasus," but I was informed that the "machine" was broken, and that the next performance would be "on Friday, if God grant"—a dark cinema-house where by the light of an oil lamp, which seemed strangely out of place, one discerned a refreshment bar, a cashier's box, where should have been a girl selling tickets, curtains separating the waiting-room from the theatre, and finally three or four hopeful or disappointed would-be customers. I asked a Russian present if he did not find in the noise of the horns something very horrifying and suggestive, and he replied testily:

"Oh, a great deal of noise, that's all. Very trying for those who would rather not hear it."

He did not feel as I did about the music at all, and his matter-of-factness rather surprised me. The horns had to me the sense of calling someone, something, and they were literally terrifying.

In a depressed state of mind I wandered back to the Hotel London, and found the landlady having a nail-to-nail fight with a woman lodger. Both sides at once claimed me as a witness—the police were coming, and I would testify. The landlady had broken into the lodger's room and told her to leave at once; the latter, a great, big, hysterical Russian woman, had replied with fisticuffs and sobs and clamour.

The landlady gave a very disparaging account of the woman lodger's present behaviour and past career. The woman lodger, under the strange impression that she possessed good looks, tried to ingratiate me to be on her side by giving me saucy looks and knowing smiles. The yard porter had been sent for the police, and all the while there were strident cries of "the police are coming"—and the horns kept up their rumpus over the city, *terumm, terumm, terumm.*

I was sorry my room had no key and that the window was shuttered from the outside. The police came and ordered that the woman be allowed to remain till the morning, and a silence settled down on the inn—silence broken only by the sound of the horns of the orchestra a mile away. All sorts of fancies possessed my mind and wrought me to a state of terror, so that I was afraid of my dreams.

What I dreamed that night has probably little to do with Russian Central Asia, and yet I shall never think of my journey across this wild and empty land without half recalling it involuntarily. Even if I believed that dreams had never any definite prophecy or foreboding in them, this one is one I should take to a dream interpreter. Now that I know that all this summer a great war was in preparation and the dogs of lust and hate were being unloosed, I can say to myself that I at least had warning that the Devil was at large, that an evil spirit had escaped into the world.

I ought, perhaps, to tell first the dream which my

friend G—— told me before I left Vladikavkaz, when he warned me of a great impending world calamity. G—— said that one night, after an arduous day's work teaching in class and coaching private pupils at home, he lay down on his couch and dozed. Hardly had he fallen asleep, when three men of Eastern aspect, dark faced, bright eyed, brown handed, with white robes from their shoulders and white turbans on their heads, appeared to him and pronounced six words in a loud, oracular voice and disappeared. A second time they appeared and did the same. A third time they appeared and pronounced them, and this time one of them took up a pen and made as if to write. The words were not Russian, or, indeed, any language which G—— knew, but after the third apparition and disappearance he wakened up with a start and at once picked up an exercise-book and wrote the words down. They were: *Imaktúr nites óides ilvéna varèn cevertae.* G—— had never been a student of the occult before, but this caused him to consider. I begged G—— to write them down for me and let me see how they looked in black and white.

"Well, what do they mean?" I asked.

"I cannot yet be sure," said G——. "They are certainly part of a language. Of that I am convinced. I have consulted many great linguists, and whilst they cannot say what language it is or where its lingual affinities are to be found, they all agree that it has the nature of real language. I have thought, as I lived in the Caucasus in the midst of so many Eastern tribes, that it might conceivably be intelligible to one or other of them. I have questioned Ingooshi, Ossetini, Khevsuri, but none recognised any likeness to any tongue they had ever heard in the mountains. I have been to Petersburg, Berlin, Paris to try and find out what the words meant, and all to no avail. Specialists were most sympathctic, but could tell me nothing. However, since then I have made a profound study of occult language, and have arrived at some understanding of the significance of the dream. All I can tell you is that a world calamity is coming, a great cataclysm or natural subversion. We may expect great earthquakes. Germany certainly is in dangcr."

The dream I had in Aulie Ata was certainly much worse than this. I thought G—— rather crazy about this dream of his at the time, and I listened incredulously to his prophecies. But if I regarded them flippantly perhaps I was wrong. Certainly, if I held there was no such verity as the occult I was wrong.

They say that Fear stands on the threshold of the occult world, and as my dream consciousness impinged upon it I expcrienced abject terror, a terror that creeps through the marrow of the bones and lifts the roots of one's hair at a thought.

I lay down in my dark room at the Hotel London at Aulie Ata after the fight between landlady and lodger had ceased but whilst the Sart orchestra still blew their horns over the city. The bed was a foot short for my tired body; the shutters of the room were barred; I had no lamp, but only a bit of candle of my own. After a fortnight spent under the stars and in the immense open house of earth and heaven, it was sufficiently oppressing and depressing in this shuttered chamber. But I was tired with the tiredness of one who has tramped under a sub-tropical sun from dawn to sunset and has added an evening of town excitement to the weariness of a long journey.

I had hardly lain down before I fell asleep. At once I began to dream. I had been invited to a friend's house, and was for a moment by myself in his dining-room; there was nothing on the table but the cruet. I was terribly thirsty, and I rushed to one of the bottles and began to drink from it, but, my host coming along the corridor and into the room, I at once put the bottle back and pretended that I had been doing nothing of the kind. This awoke me. My eyes opened, and I thought to myself: "What an absurd dream! What a dreadful thing pretending is. Why cannot we be as we are? Manners is, in a way, pretence. Every polite man who comes up to you to shake hands, if we only knew it, has been doing something the moment before as impossible as drinking the contents of the cruet. Mankind are pretenders. The spirit is truth, but the incarnation is a mask. The whole aspect of humanity is a pretending to be what it is not. . . ."

I was rather struck by the thought, but lapsed into sleep again. And then came my terrible dream. In the depths of my sleep a voice suddenly cried out the most terrifying words I think I have ever heard, and they were: "*A great dissimulator has escaped, shut in prison from everlasting.*"

At that I started up from my bed with the perspiration on my brow and the most hideous fear of the Devil. I felt that some new evil spirit was at large and was seeking a home in a man. My earlier thought came back to me—all spirits are dissimulators, whether they be devils or angels, and we men and women are all angels pretending to be men and women. But now I knew that some devil from which the world had mercifully been preserved (from everlasting) had escaped into our life, and would take the form and the appearance of a man somewhere. I had intelligence of the Antichrist. And now that we are all in the depths of this war I ask myself sometimes is there a genius of evil in all this, has the Antichrist perhaps appeared? Does not the fact that St. George and the angels (the angels, at least, of Mons) are fighting on our side suggest that the evil powers incarnate are on the other side?

It was two in the morning; the Sarts had stopped blowing their horns, there was a breathless stillness. I wakened up the hotel porter and bade him open the shutters of my windows. I lit my candle, took up pen and paper, and wrote a long letter home. I took out Vera's ikon of Martha and Mary, and put it in front of me. I looked at it and wrote—wrote, wrote. I told all the happenings of the long day past, the tramping, the sun, the far away vision of Aulie Ata, the strange town, the Sart orchestra, the Armenian garden restaurant, the Hotel London, the fight of the two women, the dream of the dissimulator. I was afraid the candle would go out before dawn. Dawn seemed a long time coming. But at last the nightingales began to sing, *p-r-r-r-r . . . sweet, sweet, sweet.* A muezzin was calling through the dark night. How resonant his voice! Somehow it went with the nightingale's song.

> A muezzin from the dark tower cries
> Fools, your reward is neither here nor there.

Again muezzins from the dark mosques of the city. Suddenly the cocks gave an extraordinary chorus, and I knew it must be near dawn, and a cart came lumbering by. Pale rents appeared through the willow trees that hid the sky. My candle grew little and yellow and flickering, but it lasted, and I wrote on and on, page after page, till it was bright morning. Then I lay down and slept an hour, and I had saved myself, perhaps, from fever. In any case, I had lived through a waking nightmare.

By day Aulie Ata was, perhaps, less mysterious, but there still remained a sense of remoteness. It was difficult to imagine European people living there all the year round and calling it "home." It is an oasis, it is true, but it might be truer to call it a sub-tropical swamp. It is fed by a mountain river, the Talass, which flows off and loses itself in the desert. But there is plenty of water and a great deal of verdure is possible, a very large settlement.

Aulie Ata has its cathedral standing in the midst

of a pleasant shadowy garden. It has its bazaar, and its trotting-ground for a horse fair and cattle market. Here were numbers of Sartish shops where bread and hot meat-pies were sold. Scores of Kirghiz on horseback or on bulls blundered about amidst cattle and mud. Young men were trying horses and showing their paces; others were making deals in sheep and goats. The sheep for sale were tied in long or short knots, threaded by the heads as Russians thread onions.

As a general rule a sheep was reckoned as being equivalent in value to a three-rouble note, and many of the Kirghiz had brought up their sheep merely as money, and when they bought six shillings' worth of stuff at some shop they detached a sheep from their coil and passed him on to the shopman. So I saw for the first time in my life the literal significance of *pecunia* as the Romans understood it.*

Aulie Ata is subject to earthquakes, and my landlady explained how one morning she was washing the floor of her establishment, bending down over her floorcloth with her legs apart, and suddenly she felt her legs going farther apart—by which lively figure she meant to explain how earthquakes are felt.

The chief sights of the city were the caravans of emigrants toiling onwards towards the farther East. Here were no farms for them, no encouragement given to settle. For there is now no particular political need for the colonisation of Sirdaria; the

* *Pecus*=a head of cattle, a beast of the field.

Russians are far more powerful than the native population, and could never be overthrown by an uprising or mutiny. The Government encourages emigration to the points where it is politically most advantageous—that is, on the very frontier lines. The most vigorous irrigation and settlement work goes on on the frontiers of China, Afghanistan and Persia. The colonists have a long road in front of them even after they have reached Aulie Ata. I myself went on with them.

The weather changed whilst I was at Aulie Ata; torrential rain came down, rain brought down by the mountains, and only deluging their own slopes and the country in the immediate vicinity. The desert twenty miles away remained, no doubt, as parched as ever. The River Talass, in flood outside the town, presented an unwonted spectacle; the wide, black, diversified, shingly river, the lowering clouds overhead, the restless wind from the mountains spitting and promising rain, the emptiness and dreariness of the world all around, except at the place where the bridge should have been—but from which it had been lately washed away—and there, an ever-increasing collection of straw or canvas tilted wagons and carts, and of oxen, camels and horses, all the caravans of the emigrants, waiting, as it were, for a ferryman to take them to another world.

I got over at last on a Kirghiz horse, and was pretty nearly soaked in the passage. On the other side was a more desolate country. It was wilder, more broken, perhaps a little greener, but there were very few farms. Even the Kirghiz seemed of a poorer and dirtier type. I bought milk at the Kirghiz tents and bread and eggs at the post stations. At one post-house I had a chicken cooked for me. The heat was not so trying on this road, for clouds had come over and rain had laid the dust. I had a sense of travelling in the opposite direction of the way of the seasons. It had been like June in Tashkent, but here it was early May. Still, the temperature in the shade must have reached 90° Fahr.

I slept three nights in the open and tramped three days before I finally passed out of the province of Sirdaria and entered the Semiretchenskaya Oblast, Seven Rivers Land, the remotest of the Tsar's dominions, remoter than the Far East, because there is no communication either by rail or river. On my right the great chain of mountains with snowy summits still stretched on, and on my left the everlasting moorland. More birds appeared on my way, partridges, bustards, snipe, eagles, cranes. Straying off the road and up to the first rising ground of the mountains were a species of little deer, called here *kosuli.* Marmots popped in and out of sand burrows, occasionally falling a prey to day-flying owls. The jerboa, with long tail and dainty, bird-like legs, was a pretty visitor, and among insects the green praying-mantis was noticeable, the cicada a nuisance, and various spiders and beetles the bane of night-tide. I was constantly warned against the hairy-legged *falanga* and a black spider (the karakurt), both of which were said to have a mortal bite, though sheep could eat them without harm. Along the road laborious and stupid-looking beetles rolled their globular homes of gathered dirt.

Slow travelling out here is very featureless, and I grew tired of tramping all day, the emptiness of the life, and the dullness of mere sun and road as companions. What was my disappointment the second noon to lose a lift that would have taken me thirty versts on at the cost of a rouble. I had just got up from a siesta under my plaid tent when a countryman came along with a cart full of clover—food for his horse—and I bargained with him and got a seat literally "in clover." We proceeded thus for a mile when we came to a mud-built caravanserai, and stopped to have tea. Up to this inn came presently another cart from the other direction. It contained all his wife's family, the people he had been setting out to see. They had had a similar impulse to come and visit him. In that way I lost my lift, and could hardly share their joy at the happy meeting.

At Merke, however, the second colonial settlement in Seven Rivers Land, I hired a *troika* to Pishpek, three horses yoked to an *arba* (a native cart), the driver a Kirghiz. This is the usual mode of travelling for Russians on business in Central Asia. The *troika* stands instead of the train. But what an impression!

The Kirghiz driver, in rags and tatters, sitting on one hip on his bare wooden driving-seat, lounging to and fro, one shoulder up, one down, flicking the three galloping horses with his whip, whistling, shouting.

The horses bounding along, neck by neck, over bump, over crevice, over chasm; up hill, down dale, never slackening (there is no brake to the wooden *arba*); coming with a great splash on to a stream, the *arba* just floating on it as the horses plunge through it; out again, up the bank; what matter stones—even milestones? What a contrast to the way I crawled along when walking!

We go along roads that are like dried-up river beds, over roads little better than mountain tracks. Ever and anon I am nearly shot out of the cup of dry clover and hay on which I am sitting. I am flung against the sides, I grasp at the stained Joseph coat of the Kirghiz, I clasp him round the shoulders.

But the Kirghiz smiles and whistles and shouts again. The horses whisper hurried secrets to one another in their rhythmical threefold devouring of space. We go not by versts or by miles, but by leagues. There are no steamboats, trains, motor-cars, aeroplanes in Seven Rivers Land, but the *troika* combines these all in one.

As we go along the level highroad the whole country behind us is blotted out from view by clouds of our dust. We never hesitate as we dash through market-places and thronged colonial villages. What matter who is in the way; the *troika* goes on straight ahead, always seeming likely to collide as we dash towards other carts or charge into passing horsemen, the averted horses' faces breathing into my face as we pass.

Young Kirghiz Brides

The way is always in the view of the snowy mountains and comparatively seldom in view of houses. It is the land of the tent dwellers, and the moors are dotted with grey pyramids and columns, the temporary dwelling-places of the nomads. Now and then a whole patriarchal family of the wanderers crosses the road on its journey from the parched plains up to the greener pasture lands of the hills. They have their tents and all their goods on camels' backs; they drive with them hundreds of head of sheep and goats and cows and mares. They ride themselves on camels, horses, bulls; their white-turbaned wives, often four to each man, ride astride of bulls, their faces uncovered, babies at their bare breasts. Brides—girls of thirteen or fourteen—ride in extraordinary state in their midst, seated on palfreys with scarlet horsecloths, themselves clad in bright cottons, their hair in many glistening black plaits, each loaded with a silver bullet to keep it from entangling with sister plaits. They also sit astride, and ride with wonderful grace, as if conscious of being the treasure of the whole caravan. They are good to look upon.

We pass endless lines of wagons drawn by toiling oxen or little, jaded ponies, and tended by burly Russian peasants and their plump, laughing, perspiring womenkind—emigrants going to settle in the youngest of Russian colonies a thousand miles or more from a railway station. We have to turn off the road and tumble over the rough moorland in order to circumvent hundreds of such emigrant wagons. We overtake and pass the equivalent of whole goods trains—long strings of lorries and pack-carts and camels, piled with consignments of goods to be delivered all along the way from Southern Siberia on the one hand and from Orenberg and Tashkent on the other to the limits of the Himalaya Mountains. We pass, or, as it happens, get entangled in a mile of camels, each having on its back a mountain of horsehair or wool, some twenty couples of dirty camels in a company, each company led by a Chinese Mohammedan on an ass, a *Dunkan.*

We pass the mud-walled, mud-domed, ace-of-spade-like tombs of the Kirghiz; we pass ruins of ancient towers, battered caravanserais. We escape from the desert into a sort of artificial oasis made by irrigation—the Russian village or Cossack *stanitza.* We change horses.

At nightfall I overtake a lady going to the town where her sweetheart lives. She is in a hurry that brooks no delay. There are only horses for one, so I offer her a place in my *arba.* She is accompanied by many boxes and bags. She wants to go on all night, no matter——

Twilight turns to darkness, the moon comes out fair and large, opposite the setting sun. The clouds are lit with gentle light and a faint colouring. The *troika* goes on and on. I lie full length in the *arba,* my head on a pillow which my companion has lent me, and I look up at the sky. The night is gentle and touching. The Kirghiz is silhouetted above us;

"PAST THE RUINS OF ANCIENT TOWERS"

the moon is now shining full upon us; in a moment it is cut off by the black line of the roof of the cart, but even then the sky is the more beautiful for a hidden presence. We sit up and look into the night landscape.

The moon gives glimmering illumination to squads of poplars, waving cornfields, silver streams, the thatched roofs of cottages, mud huts. The nightingale sings the short night through, owls hoot, dogs rush out at us as if they were fired from farm-yards, but the laconic driver flicks them with his long whip when they get near the horses' legs, and they fall each into the rear and slink back to the dark yards whence they came.

We leave behind populous villages, and issue on to the moors. Night hides the scarlet poppies, but the air contains their odours. The moon no longer stands over the black mound of the horizon, but has climbed over the zenith. The cocks are crowing, my companion is sleeping, the bells of the *troika* are chingle-dingling, chingle-dangling all the time.

We have to change horses, however. We get a samovar in the waiting time, and Zinaida—such is her name—becomes an excited chatterbox. It is only fifty miles to her goal and her sweetheart. She tells me how she met him, what sort of life they will lead when they are married, the name of their first boy, should they have one.

Two scalding glasses of tea, and then into the *arba* once more, with fresh horses, and a new Kirghiz driver wakened up to take us. Zinaida's boxes are corded on securely, her bandboxes are better bestowed away, she makes a more comfortable arrangement of quilts and pillows, and we lie back and both fall asleep.

When next we change horses sun pales the stars. It is the last change. Twenty miles more and our winged chariot flies up the courtyard of the town post-house. I am stiff. Zinaida, however, is as fresh and nimble as a young deer. A young man with a pallid face is waiting for her on the post-house steps, and she jumps down to him in a trice, and he folds her in his arms and kisses her.

We passed through Bielovodsk and Novy Troitsky, the latter being an extensive Cossack station, where all the village men have red stripes on their trousers, and where even the little boys riding the horses in from the steppe have red-striped breeches cut down from father's. The Cossacks are soldiers first and peasants only second or third. Whilst farming they are understood to be "on leave," and when war breaks out they are at once at the direct service of the Tsar on the field of battle. Novy Troitsky was a Cossack camp in the days of the conquest of Central Asia, and when pacification was consummated the Cossacks were invited to send for their sweethearts, wives, mothers, families, and settle on the pick of the land chosen out for them by the Government. There are many such settlements; they are called *stantsi*, or stations, whereas the other settlements are called *derevnyi*, villages.

On the whole, Seven Rivers Land seemed to be

more fruitful than Northern Sirdaria. The settlements were very large ones; there were many enormous villages with schools, churches, big general stores and several thousand inhabitants. Pishpek, however, was not quite so large as Aulie Ata. The populations of the colonial towns on my route may give an idea of these growing agricultural communities:

				Inhabitants
Chimkent ..	64	versts from railway station	..	15,756
Aulie Ata ..	242	" " "	..	19,052
Pishpek ..	505	" " "	..	16,419
Verney ..	743	" " "	..	31,317
Kopal ..	1,102	" " "	..	3,966
Sergiopol ..	1,352	" " "	..	2,261

These figures are taken some years ago, and probably twenty per cent. should be added to the numbers now. These are the biggest.

The towns of this colony are not connected with Western Europe either by rail or waterway, and there is an unexampled provincialism in the country. The people are far away by themselves, and they have consequently developed a distinctive local patriotism. The Central Asian pioneers are great talkers about their own country, and they are proud of everything that marks it out as different from Russia and the rest of the world. They are proud of its vast empty spaces, its mountains, its wild beasts and birds, its tigers, wild boars, aurochs, wild goats, its falcons, flamingos, partridges; proud of the Kirghiz, of the tortoises, of the camels—in fact, of anything and everything that seems to mark the country as original. Its people are all hunters. The engineer, the "topograph," the "hydro-technic," the land surveyor, the Cossack, the peasant colonist, all carry the gun. The towel-hooks and hat-pegs in their houses are goat horns and antlers. The words of the colonists' mouths run out in hunting-stories. All journeys are made on horseback or by post-horses, and the people are always moving to and fro. Even the colonists shift about from one settlement to another—by arrangement with the colonisation authorities.

I met many people on my journey: two *khodoki*, foot messengers from a village in Kursk government, sent by the villagers to spy out the land and choose a plot for colonisation, but now hastening back in order to be home by St. Peter's Day and the cutting of the barley. Land was scarce with them; all in the hands of the landowners. The population increases—so many children always are born—but the free land does not increase. The two *khodoki* had not, however, found what they wanted in Semiretchie, and were returning to Kursk with a tale of disillusionment. "They told us it was heaven out here, and you reaped harvests just after throwing out the seed. But it appears there is as much work here as there," said they.

I met a commercial traveller, a "*voyageur*, the representative of a certain firm," as he called himself. He was travelling post-horses, and had a large chest of travelling samples, which was roped on to the back of his *britchka.* He was carrying Moscow cottons in bright assortments of colours and patterns, and when he came to a town where there were ten cotton shops he went into each rapidly and deposited a complete set of his samples, and left them with the shopkeepers for an hour or so while he had his dinner and had a shave and a bath. In that way he met me, resting while the shopowners and their friends discussed his goods. Commercial travellers in tea, sugar, cotton, china, ironware and other dry goods were very frequent on the road, but were mostly Tartars or Armenians.

I also met a boy going home from the University of Kief, going home to Verney, and in a tremendous hurry to get back to his mother and the girl he left behind him a year ago. He was "agin the Government," and imagined that England was ahead of Russia in every way, and wondered what the English would not have done with Central Asia had it been theirs. "Just think of the wealth in these mountains," said he. "Just imagine it; we have not one mine in this vast territory twice the size of Germany. We have only one factory—a lemonade factory."

"Its destiny seems to be agricultural," said I.

"What is student life like at Kief?" I asked. "Do you meet together much? Are there debates, literary discussions? What's in the air?"

He could not tell me if there was anything in the air. Life was duller there than formerly. The students kept more to themselves; but they had a *Semi-retchinsky* club. All students from Seven Rivers lived together, and they had musical evenings and dances. It was pleasant; the *Semi-retchenski* were great patriots in their way.

At Pishpek I had a delightful meeting with a Government topographer—Nazimof, a man of thirty, of gentle birth, elegant, graceful, old-fashioned. I met him at an inn. I had been put into his room by a grasping landlady who would not confess she was full up and could take no more visitors. After somewhat of a "scandal," raised by the topographer, it was agreed that I should share his room. Every corner was occupied with his professional equipment—long iron map cases with padlocks, chests of instruments, tent poles, carpet chairs, rolls of canvas, boxes of books, papers and clothes.

"Excuse all this," said he. "I am taking it up into the mountains as soon as I get news that the snow has melted a little."

He explained that he was on Government service, charting maps. He was going to live the whole summer up among the mountain passes and literally bathe in snow. He would rig up his tents by the aid of the Kirghiz, hunt, shoot, survey, chart, discover, without any other fellow-European with whom to share fellowship.

We spent two days together in Pishpek, and talked of many things. His brother had been sent to Jerusalem this year by the Orthodox Palestine Society to inquire into the conditions under which the peasants journeyed and the exploitation of the aged pilgrims by the steamship company and the

Greek monks. He had brought back just such a tale of woe and of happiness as I had myself to tell after my pilgrimage. A good deal is going to be done to better the conditions of the pilgrims' journey, and there is even a proposal that the Government take the pilgrims on their own boats. I wondered whether it was worth while interfering, and I told my own experiences on that journey and gave my impression; the telling introduced me.

My new friend told me how much he wanted to get away from Seven Rivers Land and see the world. Once, as a boy on a Russian training-ship, he had landed at Newcastle, and had seen something of England—had even slept in a sailors' rest. He would like to *see* England, to come and live there, and understand the country and the nation, to see America, also Australia. He liked being up in the mountains, working by himself in the fresh mountain air, talking to chance-met Kirghiz, shooting wild goats and partridges. But by the end of the summer he would be terribly bored. He would come down from the mountains, rush into Verney, complete his maps, and then bolt for Petersburg. He thirsted for human society all the summer through.

He was always dressed in white, and wore a fez on his shaved head. He sat with me hours in a bamboo *palatka* in the one garden restaurant of Pishpek, and we talked over koumis, over roast chicken, over tea, over wine. At night, too, when he lay on a broken-down bedstead and I on a dusty divan, he prattled of his wife and children that he was sick to leave behind, and of the boy in himself which made him always seek loneliness and adventures, however much his heart bade him remain at home.

"I wouldn't change my lot, but still it is wrong to marry at twenty, as I did. There are so many partings and it is a great pain. A young man has things to do in the world, and he is bound to put his wife and family in the background; his ties are his pains. Most happy marriages are made of men of middle years, when they have made a little fortune and can take things more easily. When a stout, old man marries a young girl, moreover, there is generally a happy, healthy family."

"But surely you don't mean to say that old men are better fathers than young men?" I urged.

"Yes; they have fewer stakes in the world. They are not called on to go and chart the valleys and peaks of the Thian Shan Mountains. They know they will not be called on to fight for their country. They know they've got enough money to educate their children and keep up a good home. They are not so fretful, not so irritable as young men, but good natured, easy going, and a pretty girl can make one do what she desires."

I surmised he must have quarrelled with his wife a little just before leaving, and be sick at heart to get back home and make it up.

Pishpek, though four hundred miles from a railway station, is a promising town. The climate seemed to be a hot and dry one, though, of course, it is easy to be misled by the chances of the weather. There are long, white streets, with ranks of poplars on each side, a big market-place, a highroad of shops and colonial stores, many places where *Kvass* and aerated waters are sold, garden restaurants. There is not the atmosphere of mystery that Aulie Ata has. It is more colonial and less Eastern, though, of course, there are the inevitable Oriental hawkers and the native bazaar. Pishpek has a camel ambulance, a roughly shaped wood-sleigh with enormously long shafts, to which a Bactrian camel is yoked. Pishpek also has its lepers, and, as in all these Eastern towns, there is a great deal of skin disease, though chiefly among the natives.

The colonists seemed fairly well-to-do, though there was little evidence of culture, few books, no pianos; the cinema, it is true, but that is rather a sign of poverty. But the Russians seemed thriving and everyone seemed to have plenty of horses and cattle. In this country, where wishes are horses, even the hawker of bootlaces in the bazaar has his nag tied to a poplar tree near by.

The Kirghiz going from the parched plains up into the mountains let me understand the changing of the season. The road out from Pishpek led into desolate country, and I was troubled by the heat and the difficulty of obtaining food and drink. I carried four pounds of bread with me out of Pishpek, but that very quickly vanished, some eaten by myself, some by ants. Ants got into my bread at night and riddled it so that I could not break off a fragment without an ant appearing in it. I carried two water-bottles with me, and filled them with milk or water when I could. Neither milk nor water seemed to be very good to drink. The best thing out here is the aerated water, apricot or pineapple; it is very thirst-quenching and a good corrective to the stomach. When my European bread gave out I had to eat *lepeshka,* which I cannot recommend. It seems a possible diet when one is hungry, and if you have wine to wash it down you feel you are making a beautiful meal. One afternoon, however, I had a *très mauvais quart d' heure* after *lepeshka.* A lump of it stuck in my gullet and would not go down and could not come up. I thought I was choked.

A melancholy native stands with a tray of *lepeshki* in the road, and you buy three for five copecks—three rolls for five farthings. No matter how hard they are, they can be soaked and softened in tea. But I often wondered what gave the cement-like quality to them. On the road I have often felt that my diet was unsuitable, but never have I had such indigestion as on a diet of mare's milk and *lepeshka.* It is claimed that mare's milk is the best thing in the world for the stomach. Koumis cleanses and fortifies and freshens everything; it is the mother of the inside. But it does not dissolve *lepeshka.* I was told that it was difficult to tell the difference between champagne and mare's milk.

"But, to start with, one is white," said I.

"Oh, it's not the colour; it's the quality."

A SETTLED KIRGHIZ: ONE OF THE CHARACTERS OF PISHPEK

"It is best when it is thick."

"It's not a matter of being thick or thin, but in the tingling taste and the exuberance and happiness you feel after it."

"Well, I've nothing to say against koumis."

I kept a diary of on what and how I spent my money on the road, and the entries run like this:

	Copecks.
Monday.	
Boiling water	5
Koumis	10
	15
Tuesday.	
Boiling water	3
Lepeshka	5
Milk	5
	13
Wednesday.	
Koumis	10
Pilgrim	5
Beggar	2
Milk	10
Kvass	3
	30
Thursday.	
Lepeshka	5
Sheep's milk	5
Koumis	10
	20

And so on; a poor budget. The greatest disappointments of this journey were the absence of fuel and the great difficulty of making a fire. It took something like two hours to collect enough straw and withered grass and splinters of wood to make a fire. And the dried camel-dung blocks would not burn. As I tramped I made it a golden rule to pick up and put in my knapsack every bit of combustible material that my eye lighted upon on the road, but even so it often happened that I had to buy hot water at some dusty, broken-down caravanserai or in a Russian inn or from some Tartar draper.

Night in an inn or post-house or under the resplendent Asian stars! Hot day toiling over empty moors and across half-empty deserts, staying in shady Russian villages, going up the yards of the farmhouses with my pot in hand asking for milk, drinking about a pint of milk, and filling my two bottles so that I might have something better than water with which to quench my thirst when I was out on the road again; talking to the farmers; riding behind the reckless Kirghiz and his three horses; and then night again and its problems and charms!

Seventeen versts beyond Pishpek is Constantinovka, and seventy-one versts, Kurdai. Russian settlement is rather sparse until Kazanskaya Bogoroditsa and Linbovinskaya are reached, and these are in the urban district of Verney, the capital of the colony. There is an enormous amount of room for human beings here and, when the railway comes along and puts stations every twenty miles or so from European Russia, all the way to Kuldja in China.

Arrival at Verney

After the Cossack village of Linbovinskaya, with its shops and bazaar, comes the approach to Verney, and the high road is worn into many tracks and is broad and deep in dust. Along these come many equipages and picnic carts with pleasure parties of Russians, and for the first time since leaving Tashkent there was a suggestion of the life of a large provincial town. But, after all, Verney was only a larger Pishpek.

IX

THE PIONEERS

ALL the way to Verney the carts are travelling eastward, but on the road to Kopal two processions meet one another; the colonists coming from Tashkent meet the colonists coming from Omsk and Semipalatinsk. It struck me that those coming from the North were a poorer, harder, more jaded people than those who had accompanied me from the West. Perhaps that was because the journey from Siberia was more trying and there was less to eat on the way, or because the people who came by way of the northern road were from provinces of Russia where the standard of living and the average of health were lower.

The pioneers were a rugged sort of folk. They walked with their oxen and horses, they wandered all over the sandy wastes looking for roots and straws, and fifty people would spend hours getting enough fuel to make a fire to boil their pots. They got covered in white dust; their boots were through; their feet blistered; their carts broke down or cattle died; but still the band went on patiently, cheerily. They went very slowly, and I overtook many bands as I walked. I would fall in with the caravan at evening, and listen with an involuntary thrill to the great choruses these people sang as they went. They chaffed one another, gossiped, shouted to the cattle, sang with as much easy-going cheerfulness as if they were in their native province and driving the cattle in from their own pasture lands, and not threading the road across the silent deserts of Central Asia. I would see another party afar off at ten in the morning, a grey-brown mass on the horizon, and catch it up by twelve noon. And there would be a strange sight: not a single peasant walking or in sight. Only the creaking, slowly moving, patient carts and the clumsy, straining oxen or little ponies, going on by themselves without the flick of a whip or the whisper of a master's voice. And, coming close up to the wagons, I would hear snoring. The whole caravan would be sleeping and snoring in the shelter of the tarpaulin tilts, and yet going ever slowly on, slowly on, through the blaze of the Asian noon-day, over the desert, toward the happy valleys of the East.

I suppose that, but for the instinctive movements of the Russian people and the seeking spirit, it would be difficult for the Government to settle these remote tracts of the Russian Empire. People would not go simply because of the grants they obtain. It is the wandering spirit that is the foundation of the Empire. In Central Asia the officials complain that the people who come are not like those who remain behind in Russia; they are the most restless of all Russians. They have wandered thus far, but they have no wish to settle down even now. They take up land, build villages, till the soil, but sure enough after a few years they are itching to move on farther. The majority of colonists are people who have come not direct from Russia, but from some less remote farm or homestead in Turkestan, Seven Rivers Land, or Siberia. And these people do not recognise the arbitrary limits of the Russian Empire, but stray over in considerable numbers into Persia, Mongolia, and Chinese Tartary. It is true that the Government exercises considerable control upon the movements of the pioneers. It indicates each year what tracts of territory are open to colonisation, what developments have been made in the irrigation system, and shows spots where villages may be built. The colonial village is not a haphazard growth such as is the ordinary European village. It does not simply grow; it is planned by the Government engineers and indicated in a schedule before ever a single inhabitant has set eyes on it.

When the harvest has been taken in in Russia many peasants go on pilgrimage to shrines and many go out in quest of new land. The *khodoki*, or walkers, set out. A village or a family sends out a messenger to seek new land; this messenger is called a *khodok*. The *khodoki* are specially encouraged by the Government. The police will not allow a whole village to take to the road and go off all together in quest of land; they insist on the *khodok* going first and booking something in advance. Very great reductions are made in railway fares and great facilities are given to the *khodoki*, who go forth and look at all the valleys and irrigated levels at the disposal of the

THE IRRIGATED DESERT—AN EMBLEM OF RUSSIAN COLONISATION IN CENTRAL ASIA

colonists during the year in question. They travel in twos and threes, one *khodok* being required for each three families.

When the *khodoki* come back, after three weeks, or it may be three months, or three years, there is necessarily tremendous excitement in the village. They cannot then disclaim the *khodok's* authority to have taken land in their name, or in any case they very seldom do disclaim it. It often happens, of course, that the *khodoki* return saying that they have found nothing better than their own land and their own village, and that, consequently, they do not recommend a move. Many of the *khodoki* I met on the road were well-to-do peasants who had a stake in the old country and would not readily advise their constituent villagers to sell out and come to Central Asia. Still, more than half of the messengers sent out come back with a positive message. They have found and taken land.

Whether the *khodok* has done well or ill, the families set out. It happens occasionally that the messengers choose death-traps and places of eternal desolation, and they are terribly blamed. But it ought to be remembered that Government engineers and agricultural specialists have indicated the sites as possible before ever the *khodoki* set eyes on them; or a Russian general, visiting a district, has said: "Plant fifteen villages on the eastern slopes of this range of hills," or "twenty villages along this valley," and it has been done simply because he wanted Russian villages for strategical considerations.

The manner of settling the Empire is so interesting to us that I append a summary of the information given to all Russians desirous to emigrate to the Russian colonies. This is for the year 1914:

The provinces open to colonisation this year are those of Uralsk, Turgaisk, Akmolinsk, Semipalatinsk, Seven Rivers, Tobolsk, Tomsk, Yenisei, Irkutsk, Transbaikal, Amur, and Primorsk. Also Yakutsk, Sakhalin, and Kamchatka.

The following people are allowed to settle beyond the Ural.—All peasants and *meshtchane*, those engaged exclusively in agriculture, and also artisans, workmen, factory hands, merchants and shopkeepers. People of other classes must, before emigrating, apply to the governor of the province in which they live.

The Government invites no one to emigrate, and is anxious only to show all possible help to those who have decided to take that step, and to make the emigration laws and the grants and privileges accorded to colonists clear to everyone.

EMIGRATION OF AGRICULTURISTS

All agriculturists thinking of crossing into Asia should first think well: Is there not some way of improving the home land and remaining on it?

Having become owners of your land at home (by the completion of purchase after the liberation from serfdom), it is possible to let part of it out to others, or by careful culture greatly increase the harvest, or you can mortgage it to the Peasants' Bank and buy other land, either in your own or in a neighbouring province.

It is another matter when the land you possess is so little that there is none to let out or mortgage, or when it is difficult to buy suitable land at all near, when the land offered by Government or private owners becomes year by year less and the prices year by year higher.

Then it is worth while considering the question of emigration to Asiatic Russia, where there is still much space. The Government assigns land to the extent of 25-50 dessiatinas a farm or 8-15 dessiatinas for each male soul. Or it is possible to settle in a village or Cossack station by special arrangement, and lease land cheaply from settled colonists. To enable people to travel to such places the Government helps with cheap tariffs and money grants.

During the past seven years more than three million souls have firmly established themselves in this way, and in many places it may be said that the colonists have become rich and live in a more flourishing way than they did on the old lands at home. But it must be remembered that such results are not attained at once. It is not a little heavy labour, grief and poverty that have to be undergone during the first years in the new place. Not every family has the strength to bear such trial. It is reckoned that of every hundred families going across the Ural fifteen return to the old country after having failed to take root in the new. It is hard for families where the general health is weak, where there are not good working hands, or where there is no money whatever to start with. Such families would do better not to stir; better to work a bit more on the home lands till they get some means to take up new land and try and develop it.

THE EMIGRATION OF FACTORY HANDS AND ARTISANS

The towns and villages are greatly in need of people knowing trades. Especially great is the need in the provinces of Amur, Primorsk, and Trans-baikal, where railways, fortresses, and barracks are being built, and where mining, fishing and lumbering are in full swing. More than a hundred thousand men are employed annually on the Government works alone, and private firms want more. Unskilled labourers, brickmakers, joiners, diggers, bricklayers, sawyers, locksmiths, glaziers, miners, and anyone who has any special knowledge or knack, willing hands and a heart to work.

Wages are higher than in European Russia, and all manner of help is given in transport. There is a great reduction of fares on the Siberian Railway, and every *artel* of workmen contracted for the Government, and also for many private businesses in connection with lumbering and fisheries, is transported to its field of work FREE OF CHARGE and taken back at specially cheap rates.

Many of those who go out with *artels* like the

country and the conditions so much that they prefer to stay and take up plots of land and settle.

WHERE AND HOW IS IT POSSIBLE TO SETTLE?

In the provinces open for colonisation there are a great number of specially chosen plots of Government land at the disposal of individuals or of numbers electing to farm and work together. The names of peasants electing to see these or choose one of them are gratuitously enrolled by the emigration officials. In the more settled and inhabited places of Siberia, Turkestan and Seven Rivers Land, where land has now obtained a considerable value, there are also special plots marked out by the Government, and these may be bought. Also in many peasant settlements and Cossack stations there are wide stretches of land granted by the Government to the Cossacks or sold in time past to freed serfs, and on these it is possible to settle when arrangements can be made privately with the peasants or the Cossacks, as the case may be. Finally, it is also possible to lease land or to buy it from private individuals.

TO WHOM DOES THE GOVERNMENT GIVE HELP?

Although emigration is permitted to all who wish, yet, in order to enjoy the advantages of Governmental help and grants in aid, it is necessary that families should first send out messengers, and should await their return before setting out themselves. This is only enforced by the Government in order to save the people from the ruin which often follows unconsidered and frivolous emigration. It should be remembered that all who have not obtained land in advance through their messengers (*khodoki*) will find that they have to take their turn last in the selection of plots of land.

THE SENDING OF MESSENGERS (KHODOKI)

Any peasant or town family occupying itself with agriculture can now send out a *khodok*, and it is now allowed to send one *khodok* to represent several families, but not more than five. What is more, any working man, artisan or tradesman can obtain a *khodok's* certificate without difficulty, and can make the journey to the places of colonisation and become acquainted with the local conditions.

The faithful *khodok* should make a thorough study of conditions of life in the new places, consider carefully all the plots of land offered, and, choosing the most suitable, inscribe his name for it according to the regulations. The *khodok* must not set off without his certificate, for only by showing the certificate can he travel at reduced rates or be recognised by the officials in Turkestan or Siberia.

In Seven Rivers Land and the other provinces of Turkestan no permission is given to people of other than the Russian race or the Orthodox religion. In the case of Old Believers and other sects whose teaching forbids military service, no permission can be granted to settle—therefore, no Molokans, Baptists or Seventh Day Adventists are allowed to settle anywhere in Turkestan.

The Most Convenient Time

The certificates, both for *khodoki* and emigrating families, are given gratuitously. The *khodok* certificate for 1913 is printed on yellow paper, the colonists' on rose-coloured paper, and the tariff certificate on green.*

The most convenient time for looking over the plots of land is from April till June, but the best are taken up very quickly at the beginning of spring; many people of foresight get to the various points in the winter in order to form an idea of the winter life of the district and to be on the spot when the new plots are laid open in the early spring.

In order to make it easier for the messengers and to decrease the expense, *khodoki* are advised to go in groups and not alone. A party together always fares better than separate people can, and more trouble is necessarily taken for them.

Khodoki often take very little money with them, and, through poverty, are obliged to return without having found the land they want. It is not possible to find suitable land at once; it is necessary to go to various places and look at many farms. For that, time and money are both necessary.

It is not thought wise to answer advertisements or apply at offices where the promise of arranging everything is made. It is impossible to take up land except through application to the emigration officials, and they do their work without making any charge. Everyone who promises to obtain an option on a plot

* This differentiation in hue is in case the persons holding the certificates should be illiterate.

of Government land after the payment of a fee is practising deceit, and complaint should be lodged at the Emigration Department in St. Petersburg. (Postal address: St. Petersburg Emigration Department, Morskaya 42. Telegraphic address: St. Petersburg, Emigrant.)

Khodoki should remember that many of the free plots of land indicated in the booklet may have been allotted to other people before their arrival. So it is, generally speaking, wise to take a wide view of the possible places of settlement. *Khodoki* should obtain the full list of plots offered by the Government. This list can be obtained at Seezran station, at Orenberg, Iletsk, Ak-bulak, Jurun, Arees, Tashkent.

The following reductions are made in railway and steamer fares for messengers and colonists and their families, and also in the charges for baggage:

1. People holding certificates as colonists or messengers of colonists are taken on all railways at a reduced fare—at a fourth of the cost of a third-class ticket—and they are accommodated in the grey wagons of the fourth class, or, in the absence of these, in goods trains. Children up to ten years of age are carried free.

2. Baggage is taken on the same train as that by which the colonists travel, and is charged at the rate of one hundredth part of a farthing per pood per verst, the first pood per ticket going free. Horses and horned cattle are taken at half a farthing per head per verst, and small domestic animals at a quarter of a farthing per head per verst. Fowls and

small animals in cages or baskets are charged by weight as if they were ordinary baggage.

3. Baggage is divided into three categories.

First category.—Domestic goods and furniture in packing cases; more than eight poods per person of either sex cannot be taken at this rate.

Second category.—Animals, carts, agricultural machinery, guns, provisions, can only be taken to the number and extent shown on the back of the tariff certificate.

Third category.—Grain, flour, seed, trees and vines can only be taken up to ten poods per person.

Beyond these limits baggage must be taken at the general commercial tariff.

In the case of loss the railway undertakes to pay the owner forty roubles a pood for baggage in the first category (though not more than 120 roubles for each ticket), six roubles a pood for the second category, and a rouble and a half a pood for the third category.

TABLE OF DISTANCES

	Versts.	Approximate equivalent in miles.
From St. Petersburg to—		
Omsk	2,937	1,958
Semipalatinsk	3,666	2,444
Tashkent	3,727	2,484
Vladivostock	8,268	5,512
From Moscow to—		
Omsk	2,681	1,794
Semipalatinsk	3,410	2,340
Tashkent	3,123	2,082
Vladivostock	8,012	5,340

TABLE OF DISTANCES (*continued*)—

From Odessa to—		*Versts.*		*Approximate equivalent in miles.*
Omsk ..	..	3,784	..	2,522
Semipalatinsk	..	4,513	..	3,008
Tashkent ..	..	4,536	..	3,024
Vladivostock	..	9,115	..	6,076

TABLE OF RAILWAY FARES FOR EMIGRANTS

No. of versts.		*Equivalent in miles.*		*Cost of ticket in roubles.* *rbls.*	*copks.*		*Equivalent in shillings.** *s.*	*d.*
750	..	500	..	1	80	..	2	8
1,500	..	1,000	..	2	80	..	4	2
2,250	..	1,500	..	3	65	..	5	5
3,000	..	2,000	..	4	45	..	6	7
3,750	..	2,500	..	5	55	..	8	3
4,500	..	3,000	..	6	65	..	9	11
5,250	..	3,500	..	7	65	..	11	5
6,000	..	4,000	..	8	75	..	13	0
7,500	..	5,000	..	10	95	..	16	4
9,000	..	6,000	..	13	05	..	19	7

BAGGAGE TARIFF FOR EMIGRANTS

To carry 3 poods (i.e. 1 cwt.)—

1,000 versts .. 30 copecks (i.e. about 6d.)
5,000 „ .. 1 rouble 50 copecks (2s. 3d.).
9,000 „ .. 2 roubles 70 „ (4s.).

To carry 30 poods (i.e. ½ ton)—

1,000 versts .. 3 roubles (4s. 6d.).
5,000 „ .. 15 „ (22s. 6d.).
9,000 „ .. 27 „ (40s. 6d.).

And other amounts and distances proportionately.

* Counting the rouble as worth 1s. 6d. At the moment of writing it is worth rather less than 1s. 4d., but it should improve somewhat.

Tariffs

Charges on the Rivers

From Omsk to—		*Fare in roubles. rbls. copks.*		*Baggage per pood.*
Pavlodar	..	3 20	..	20 copecks
Semipalatinsk		4 80	..	25 „
From Krasnoyarsk to—				
Batenei..	..	2 50	..	16 „
Minusinsk	..	2 80	..	18 „

At the larger stations and piers colonists' shelters have been built; free medical aïd is given, and hot food is served out cheap (for instance, a plate of lenten or of ordinary soup, four copecks—one penny).

To children up to ten years of age and to sick persons, hot food is given free. To small children (up to three years), white bread and milk is given free.

People who become ill of infectious diseases are removed to the Government hospitals and treated free.

At the great emigration stations beware of swindlers and charlatans, of whom there are not a few. It goes without saying that even the poorest emigrants have a little money, and they stand to lose even that if they are not careful. Beware of loiterers, card games with unknown persons, pick-pockets, robbers. Hide your money in a place where it cannot be stolen. Do not accept drinks of vodka or beer from unknown people. It is a common trick to scatter thorn-apple seed in vodka; the colonist loses consciousness, and is robbed. Many people have suffered in this way through lack of caution.

If on the road you purchase cattle or horses, obtain a certificate of purchase, or else the persons from whom you have bought may come back and declare that you have stolen what you bought.

SEVEN RIVERS PROVINCE (*Semiretchenskaya Oblast*)

One of the most remote Central Asian possessions of Russia, remarkable for its natural wealth and the beauty of Nature.

The route thither is either by rail to Tashkent or by rail to Omsk, and up the River Irtish to Semipalatinsk, and then 500 to 1,000 versts or more by road.

It is bounded on the south and east by China, on the north by the province of Semipalatinsk, on the west by the provinces of Sirdaria and Ferghan.

The principal inhabitants are wandering Kirghiz, of whom there are about one million. The Russians number about 200,000, and there are about 200,000 of other races. Half the Russian population is Cossack.

The province is divided into the jurisdictions of Verney, Pishpek, Przhevalsk, Jarkent, Kopal and Lepsinsk.

The northern districts of Lepsinsk and Kopal are specially suitable for agricultural settlement, and there is much land there not needing irrigation, as there is comparatively much water.

In the districts of Verney, Jarkent and Pishpek

irrigation is generally necessary. Free plots of land are mostly in the district of Jarkent and on the frontier of China. When the railway has been brought across to Verney, trade will certainly develop, so the sale of products will be facilitated and the conditions of farming very profitable.

Then the southern parts of the province are very mountainous. Fruitful valleys are separated by great ranges, but with time a road system will be developed and this difficulty overcome.

A railway will soon be built from Tashkent to Verney.

There are as yet no steamers. The largest river, the Ili, crosses the centre of the province. Besides the Ili there are many mountain streams and also large lakes; among the latter may be named Balkhash, Alakul, Issik-Kul.

The climate is very varied, there being levels of eternal snow and of burning sand. The chief occupations of the colonists are cattle farming and all branches of agriculture. A well-watered farm gives, as a rule, a rich and abundant harvest.

Wheat is sown (from 7 to 10 poods the dessiatina), rye oats (8 to 14 poods), millet, peas, potatoes, maize, sunflowers, mustard, flax, hemp, poppy, buckwheat, etc. And the harvest gives wheat up to 150 poods the dessiatina, oats give from 70 to 120 poods the dessiatina, and barley 90 poods. In the districts of Pishpek, Jarkent and Verney rice is sown, and gives 100 roubles the dessiatina clear profit. Orchards are cultivated almost everywhere with success.

PRICES

Wheat	30 to 80 copecks the pood.
Rye	30 to 60 " "
Oats	30 to 60 " "
Barley	30 to 70 " "
A horse costs ..	45 roubles
A cow costs ..	25 to 30 roubles
A camel costs ..	50 roubles
A sheep costs ..	3 to 5 roubles
Labour costs ..	from 70 copecks to 1 rouble 50 copecks the day.

GOVERNMENT GRANTS

(*a*) In the measure of 100 roubles the family is given in the districts of Pishpek and Verney, except for certain special districts where colonisation proceeds without loans. A hundred roubles are also given to settlers in the district of Kopal, excepting the survey of Altin-Emel and certain plots in the valley of the River Chu and also in the neighbourhood of the Lake Issik-Kul.

(*b*) In the measure of 200 roubles the family in the northern parts of the district of Jarkent and in the survey of Altin-Emel in the district of Kopal.

In the southern and eastern frontier region half the loan is reckoned as not returnable to the Government.

In the artificially watered tracts in the districts of Verney and Pishpek no grants are made.

Beyond personal loans special grants are made for purposes of supplying general needs, for the building of schools, churches, village barns, mills, brick factories and irrigation works. For the poorer districts the Government takes upon itself the burden of building schools and churches, and hundreds of thousands of roubles are spent annually for this purpose. The Government also sinks wells for the colonists.

Personal loans are repayable by instalments after five years. The first five years there is no need to repay anything, but during the succeeding ten years after that the whole should be cleared off.

General loans are repayable within ten years.

TAXES

Settlers are free of all Governmental charges and taxes for the first five years. During the second five years half has to be paid, and after ten years settlers take their stand with the established colonists.

MILITARY SERVICE

Settlers over 18 years at the time of settlement are allowed to postpone their starting service for three years.

In Turkestan six years' grace is given to all over 15 years of age.

TIMBER

When there is no timber, the Government provides free wood for building purposes—from the nearest Crown forest.

TURKESTAN

Though, generally speaking, Turkestan is shut for the purposes of immigration, nevertheless a great number of people go there every year, there being a great demand for labour of all kinds. Cotton growers give even as much as two roubles fifty copecks per day. Good wages are paid on the irrigation works. Artisans are needed in the towns and villages. Turkestan is rich, and can support any working man who goes there. It is good to go there and make some money before taking up land, and also to get some experience of the climate and conditions. As regards the taking up of land when allowed, grants in the measure of 165 roubles are given in the provinces of Sirdaria, Samarkand and Ferghan, and in the measure of 250 roubles to settlers in the frontier regions of Zaalaisk and Pamir, half of which is not returnable.

It is impossible to give the whole of this "combined circular" in extenso, but I think I have included or summarised all that is vital. It indicates the scaffolding of empire building. The people at home feel cramped or restless. They send out their *khodoki*, the pioneer messengers. The messengers select a portion of new land and return to Russia. The families of the emigrants follow. But first they must sell off or abandon all manner of cumbersome property; and good-bye has to be said to friends, to the old village, to church and churchyard, and the dead. Most difficult of all for many Russians is the

THE SHADY VILLAGE STREET—ONE LONG LINE OF WILLOWS AND POPLARS

leaving the dead behind. There is the whole agony of separation, the being cut off from Russia and going forth as a new child into Siberia or Central Asia. Then the long, monotonous train journey, and the road journey at the end of it; the caravan on the Central Asian road, and it is in the caravan that the colonists begin to taste of new life, and many feel they would like to go on wandering so all their lives. But they reach the place the messenger has found for them, and then commences the great work of making a habitation of man where no habitation has ever been before. Prayers and thanksgiving, and then work. There is no possible living without work, and the rather easy-going ways of the old land have to be given up and a new life begun of arduous labour and unflagging energy. To their aid comes hope and the passion for making all things new. No Russian would work so much were it not interesting; it is real life, the wine of experience.

First of all, trees are planted. How pathetic to see the long rows of three-foot-high poplar shoots and willow twigs! A month on this sun-beaten road leaves no doubt in the emigrant's mind as to what is the first necessity—shade, shade. Trees are planted all along the main Government dyke. The colonist chooses the place for his house; he digs a trench all round it and lets in water from the dyke, and he plants trees along the trench. Then he buys stout poplar trunks and willow trunks, and makes the framework of his cottage. He interlaces little willow twigs, and makes the sort of wilted green, slightly shady, slightly sunny house that children might put up in a wood in England. But that is only the beginning. To the willow house he slaps on mud puddings. This is the filthiest work. He makes a great quantity of mud, and treads it up and down with his bare feet till he gets the consistency he requires, and then, with his hand, fetches out sloppy lumps of it and builds his walls. In a few days the mud hardens, and he has a shady and substantial dwelling, and one that in an earthquake will swing but will not collapse. His roof he makes of prairie grass, great reeds ten feet to fifteen feet in length and thick and strong, or of willow twigs again and turf. In his second year he has a little hay harvest on his roof. He ploughs his little bit of desert. He exchanges some of his oxen for cows. He strives with all his power—as does a transplanted flower—to take root. He looks forlorn. You look at his poor estate and say: "It is a poor experiment. The sun is too strong for him; he will just wither off, and the desert will be as before." But you come another day and you see a change, and exclaim: "He has taken root, after all; there is a shoot of young life there, tender and green." Along the road I noticed villages of all ages; of this year, of last year, of four years gone, of twenty years, forty years.

There are now several thousand Russian villages in Central Asia—year by year scores of new names creep into the map in faint *italics*. It is astonishing to English eyes, because we are accustomed to think that maps of Asia do not change. We like to preserve the old Asiatic names of places, and our map-makers seem to have prejudice in favour of Teuton nomenclature similar to the prejudice for spelling the names of Russian places with German pronunciation equivalents. Asia becomes predominantly Russian, and not by virtue of troops stationed at outlandish posts, but by virtue of this process of settling.

The process of colonisation is, however, slower than the process of colonising the British Empire. The population is said to increase at a greater rate, but the organic development is slower. The facilities for getting to Siberia and Central Asia are greater, but the prospect held out is not so alluring, not so fascinating. There is more work to be done by the immigrant here than in Canada or Australia or Africa. There are no large fortunes to be made in a few years, no speculative chances, no great whirling wheel of life set going. On the other hand, Russian colonisation is sounder colonisation, more solid and lasting. It has a better quality and it promises more for the future, unless we British are going to wake up to the facts of our situation.

X

FELLOW-TRAVELLERS

IT is not necessary to say much about Verney, the capital of Seven Rivers Land. It is so subject to earthquakes that it is difficult to see in it a permanent capital. No houses of two storeys can with safety be built, so it is more suited to remain a military centre and fortress than to be a great city. In order to look imposing, shops and stores have fixed up sham upper storeys; that is, they have window-fronts up above, but no rooms behind the fronts. Singer and the cinema are here, though an enormous number of Singer shops have been compulsorily closed all over the Russian Empire during the war. Verney has its bazaar, its inns and doubtful houses, its baths, dance halls, clubs, restaurants. Although it is so far from a railway station and such an enormous distance from the wicked West, it has its frivolity and sin and small crime. It has no electric cars. It has no Bond Street or West End. One may say, however, that it has its Covent Garden. Verney is a great market for fruit and vegetables. Its native name means the city of apples, and for apples it is famous. All travellers from China are given Verney apples when they pass through. Carts heaped high with giant red radishes are driven through the town, and the strawberry hawkers make many cries. Many horses are adorned with fancy garments, and I noticed donkeys with trousers on. Women ride about astride, and are evidently used to horseback, tripping along leaning forward over the horse as it springs to a gallop, sedately coming up the high street at a walk, erect like little fat soldiers. Then, Kirghiz women astride of bulls are to be seen, and I saw one carrying twin babies and yet on bull-back, dexterously holding the cord from the ring in the animal's nose, and guiding it whither it should go. Verney has its newspaper. It has some hope of culture, and in the High School two dozen students matriculate each year and go off to the Universities of Kief, Moscow, and so on. Verney folk are grumblers at home, but when they get to Russia they develop great local patriotism and sigh for a bit of Verney bread, even of the stale bread of Verney. At the Universities the students of Seven Rivers Land keep together, and know themselves as a body having certain views and opinions of their own. Then, after their course, they come back to their home land and bring tidings of Russia. I talked with some students, and found them not unlike our own colonial students in their outlook and their attitude to the Empire. They help, but, of course, a far away place like this needs a lot of helping in the matter of culture. They bring back books and musical instruments. When I went out at night, strolling through the moon-illuminated city, I listened to the tinkling of pianos, and it was interesting to reflect that each instrument, besides coming thousands of miles by train, had also come five hundred miles in a wagon along these Central Asian roads.

There is a suggestion of America in the life out here. When you ask the way you are directed by blocks, not by turnings, and you may be sure the town is a planned one, with the streets running at right angles to one another. Only Nature, with her earthquakes, has tumbled it, given you chasms to jump over, and made it dangerous to walk in the outskirts of the town at night. There is much advertisement of wares and of persons, and a keenness to prosper and get rich. "Getting rich flatters your self-esteem," I read, and again, "Buy Indian tea and get rich." It is quite clear to me that buying Indian tea really makes poorer, for it is altogether inferior to Russian tea; but, then, these people have not our experience, they do not know the history of tea-drinking in England; how once we also had good tea, but that, in the national passion for cheapness and "getting rich," we have come to drink popularly that vile thick stuff we now call tea. Verney has its rich bourgeois—rich for Verney—men with ten or twenty thousand pounds capital. Among such is, or was (for perhaps he has been interned or expelled), a German sausage-maker, who started his career in the market-place with five pounds of sausages on a plate, and is now a respected merchant with shops and branch shops and a fame for sausages throughout Central Asia.

The local newspaper had made some sort of record

THE CATHEDRAL OF ST. SOPHIA AT VERNEY—AFTER THE EARTHQUAKE OF 1887

of the cinema films that were shown in the five towns of Seven Rivers and analysed them in this way:

Scientific	2 per cent.
Historical	8 „
Industrial..	8 „
Nature	4 „
Farce	20 „
Lurid drama	60 „
Polite drama	8 „

Which seemed to give a fair account of its civilising force. I visited three or four cinemas at various remote places, and was astonished at the French and Italian horrors, German and Scandinavian bourgeois funniosities, ghastly white-slave tragedies, and many visualised penny dreadfuls. When you see the crowds of Russians at these performances you realise that the penny dreadful is by no means played out, that many people did not in the old times read the penny dreadful just because they did not know what lay between the covers of those badly printed books, what enthralling rubbish. The business has changed hands commercially, but the thing sold is the same. It is sold in a more acceptable form—that is all.

Astonishing to see the yellow men of Asia staring at the cinema: the turbaned Sart; the new Chinaman, with cropped pigtail; the baby-like Kirghiz. Whatever do they make of American business romances and the Wild West and Red Rube and Max? They seem engrossed, smile irrelevantly, stare, go out, but always come again. The cinema is a queer window on to Europe and the West.

The road from Verney to Iliisk, on the River Ili, seemed more deserted than the road to Verney had been. Many parties of pioneers evidently turn south at Verney, and not so many turn north-east towards Iliisk. It is waste territory, overgrown with coarse grass and thistles. There are occasional mountain rivulets, bridged on the roadway with straw and mud bridges much higher than the level of the road, so that every bridge is a sort of hump. Behind me and behind Verney immense steep mountains lifted themselves up into the clouds. The road that I walked was a slowly descending tableland.

I passed through the little village of Karasbi, and then through the more substantial settlements of Jarasai and Nikolaevski. These are prolonged and attenuated villages. The oldest houses are the biggest and the deepest in trees, they have plenty of out-houses and farm buildings; but the newest are bare and wretched, with poplar shoots in front of them but three feet high. There are some deserted hovels—even a fine house was perhaps a hovel to begin with, a temporary mud hut put up to give shelter whilst the first work was done on the fields. I saw many houses half built, showing their framework of yet green willow and poplar twigs. I saw whole families and villages at work on new settlements, and also families living in tents. On the foundations of the new dwellings or attached to the rude framework were little crosses, only to be taken down when there would be a place in the house for the ikons brought from their old homes in Russia. Some colonists, on being asked when they had arrived, replied, "Last week," others said, "During these days"; the dust on their wagons was new. Everyone had a sort of Swiss Family Robinson air, as of exploring an island, making natural discoveries, and bringing things from a wreck. Some groups, however, were already busy sowing their new fields, and I understood that that was the first thing to do; that was the work, and the building the new cottages was the play. They had nothing to fear from sleeping in the open every night of summer and early autumn—a lesson to these Russians, who in their home cottages or in railway carriages are afraid of fresh air as if it brought pestilence.

I spent two wonderful nights under the stars on the road to Iliisk, the first in a sort of natural cradle in a copse, the second in a hollow which I made for my body in the bare sand of the desert. I passed out of the new land on to the waste of the Ili valley; the road was visible twenty or thirty miles ahead, and on it in front of me are telegraph poles unlimited, at first with spaces between, but in the distance thick, like black matches stuck close together in the sand. I walked a long way in the evenings, and I remember, as the sun set, an enormous and foolish bustard that was under the impression I was chasing it. It would fly the space of five telegraph poles, I'd walk the space of three; then it would fly three, I'd catch up; and it would fly on ahead along the track as if it dared not desert the poles. Finally, however, just at the last rays of sunset, it flew crossways over the desert and disappeared.

I was rather nervous at this time about the *karakurt*, the black spider that sheep eat with pleasure, but whose bite is mortal to men; and each night when I made my fresh-air couch I took pains to keep out of the way of flies, beetles, spiders, and snakes. I never was troubled by the *karakurt*, but I had a lively time with beetles and running flies, to say nothing of snakes, whose sudden darts and writhings gave me momentary horrors many times. The valley of the Ili is a wild place, with tigers and panthers; a splendid district for study and sport, I should say. However, no beasts came and snuffed my face in the night.

Each night on the road I learned to expect the moon later and later. It always seems unpunctual, always late, but not worried, and having that irreproachable beauty that excuses all faults. She came up late over the Ili desert in a wonderful orange light, and then, emerging into perfect brilliance, paled the myriad stars, set them back in the sky,

> Divesting herself of her golden shift and so
> Emerging white and exquisite.

I lay looking eastward on the sand, and on my right, in the vague night shadow, lay the tremendous pyramids of the Ala Tau mountains, the great cliff triangles south of Verney, first vision of the mighty Thian Shan. The clouds had lifted off them during the night, and in the morning I saw them in their true perspective, vague, smoke-like, shadow-based and grey-white, sun-bathed, many-pointed rocky and precipitous summits stretching a hundred miles and more from east to west.

It was ten miles in to breakfast at Iliisk. The water in the little lakes being salt, and my water-bottles empty, I could not make tea. The lakes and ponds remind you that you are between Issik-Kul and Balkhash. It is, however, desert country till you come to the thickets of the river, and there the cuckoo is calling, there are bees in the air, and it is glorious, fresh, abundant summer. The bases of the mountains are all deep blue as the sky, but utterly soft and delicious to the gaze, and the colour faints into the whiteness of the hundred-mile-long line of snow.

Iliisk is marked large on the map for convenience sake. One must mark it large to indicate a town on the River Ili, but though there is a prospect of its becoming an important trade centre, it is as yet insignificant, no more than a village, a church, a post-station, a market-place, and the dwelling-houses of two thousand people. I noticed new colonists here, using their horses to tramp great slops of mud to the proper consistency of mud dough for making the walls of new cottages. So Iliisk is increasing in size, its population is growing. Most of the houses here were mud huts of the swinging kind, built to withstand earthquakes, and their roofs were very light and beautiful, being of jungle reeds of a golden colour, each stem twelve feet long and ending in a broom of soft plumage. The River Ili, from which these reeds are cut, is a grateful sheet of silver, the breadth of the Thames at Westminster, has pink cliffs, is spanned by a wooden bridge, and has little tree-grown islets. Among the reeds on the banks lurk the tiger and panther and many snakes. Little steamers go to and fro out of China and into China, doing trade in wool, but held up every now and then by the Chinese for extra bribes. In the village wagons and camels are being loaded with raw wool—indicating the future significance of the little town as a trade centre. The population is predominantly Russian, though there are Tartars, Kirghiz, and Chinese Mohammedans. Near the market-place is a Tartar mosque with a green crescent on the top of it.

My road lay eastward toward Kopal, but before taking it I had my breakfast at Iliisk—sour milk and stale bread—at a cottage, with Christ's blessing, and how good!

The morning was very hot when I set out again, and I took off my jacket and put it in my knapsack, carrying the enlarged and weighty bundle on thinly covered shoulders. The land was sandy and desolate, being too high above the level of the River Ili to allow of simple irrigation. If it is to be opened up for colonisation, the river must be tapped much higher up, in Chinese territory, but this the Chinese will not as yet allow. I met no colonists on my road out from Iliisk, not even any Kirghiz. Summer had scorched away whatever grass the desert had yielded, and the nomads had retired for the season and gone to fresher pastures higher in the hills. How frugally it is necessary to lunch in these parts may be guessed. It is no place to tramp for anyone who must have dainties and must have change. On the whole I do not recommend Central Asia for long walking tours. For one thing, there is very little opportunity of getting anything washed, including oneself; no early morning dip, no freshness. It is not as in the Caucasus:

> The wild joy of living, the leaping from rock up to rock,
> The strong rending of boughs from the fir tree, the cool,
> silver shock
> Of the plunge in the pool's living water.

At night I was fain to discard my sleeping-sack, those two sheets sewn together on three sides; but the beetles and spiders and mosquitoes made that impossible. On the other hand, the whiteness of the sack, when the moon shone full on me, always made it possible that some long-sighted Kirghiz might bring his tribe along to find out what I was.

After a night in the desert above Iliisk I came to a place which was not a place and was called Chingildinsky, perhaps because of the sound of the bells on horses galloping through, for scarce anyone ever stops there, but I suppose really after Chingiz Khan. However, at the Zemsky post-station, to which I had repaired to have tea, I made an interesting acquaintance, a M. Liamin, a Government engineer, architect, and inspector of bridges. He was travelling on a long round through Seven Rivers and Western China via Chugachak—a military-looking gentleman in the uniform of a colonel, but much more sociable than a Russian officer is permitted to be. He was riding in his own *tarantass*, with his own petted horses, Vaska and Margarita. He asked me if I would care to accompany him, and we travelled a whole day together, all day and all night. Whenever we came in sight of any game the Kirghiz coachman took his master's gun and had a shot at it. In this way we brought down two pheasants and a woodcock, to the delight of the Kirghiz and the not unmingled pleasure of his master, who could not bear to think of animals in pain. Liamin was inspecting Government buildings, chiefly bridges, and of these chiefly bridges long since washed away. He had to report annually to the governor of Semiretchie.

"There are two hundred bridges needing repair or rebuilding. I make my report, and the governor sets aside two hundred roubles. A rouble apiece," he explained, smiling. "But what is a rouble!"

We passed through remarkably empty country, but it was on this second day out of Iliisk that I met for the first time the colonists coming southwards from Siberia. More than half my journey was done; I was nearer Omsk than Tashkent.

In Liamin's *tarantass* were all manner of boxes and padlocked safes, map rolls, instruments, pillows, quilts, weapons. There was a soft depth where one sat and lolled on one's back whilst one's knees in front were preposterously high. It was a jolly way to travel, and we were both sick of solitude and glad to hear the sound of our own voices. Liamin was charming. We talked on all manner of themes. His favourite authors were Jack London, Kipling, and Dickens. Wells depressed his soul, because he was so pessimistic. It seemed to him very terrible that it was necessary to kill so many people before Man would make up his mind to live aright. The World Republic was not worth the price paid. He had read "The World Set Free" in a Russian translation, and he could not bring himself to believe that there would ever be such slaughter as a world-war meant. Mankind was not so stupid.

Though he was a high-placed official, Liamin was all against the colonisation of Central Asia, which he called a fashionable idea, and full of sympathy for the wandering Kirghiz, who were being excluded from all the good pasture lands and harried across the frontier into China. At one village where we stopped we met a land surveyor and an old, grizzled, retired colonel who both held the opposite view, and they belaboured Liamin as we sat round the samovar.

"The Kirghiz are animals, nothing more. The Russians are men. The Kirghiz are going to China. God be with them! Let them go! Are they not pagans? We should be well rid of them! Just think of their cruelty; they put a ring through a bull's nose and tie him by that to a horse, and by his tail to a camel! If they want to stay with us, let them remain in one spot, become civilised, and obtain proper passports; then their land will be secured to them. But if they *must* wander about like wild animals, here to-day and the other side of the mountain to-morrow, then they must pay for their liberty and wildness."

A grievous question, this, in Russian Central Asia. Liamin could not make his way in his argument against the colonel. The future of the Kirghiz tribes is problematical, but I should say that they were certain to go over the frontier into China in ever greater numbers as Central Asia becomes civilised by the Russians. What they will do when Mongolia and China become civilised I do not know. But that is looking a long way ahead.

At a place called Karachok we saw somewhat of the festivity of a Kirghiz wedding. There was a great crowd of men—the guests from the country round about—and they all stood around the tent of the bridegroom, while the womenfolk, apparently all collected together, sat within and improvised songs. The felt was removed from the side of the tent and the cane framework was exposed, so the girls and women within, all in white and with white turbans on their heads, looked as if they were in a cage. Kirghiz women are not veiled. They were all sitting on the floor—that is, on carpets on the ground of the tent. They sang as the Northern Russians sing in the provinces of Vologda and Perm and Archangel, in wild bursts and inharmonious keening. The men

VISITORS AT A KIRGHIZ WEDDING

joined occasionally in the songs, and occasionally burst into laughter, for the words werc full of funny things invented by the girls. That seemed to be the sum of the entertainment. A sheep had been roasted whole. A race had been run for the prize of a dead goat—the national *baiga* race. About midnight the singing ended, and the guests prepared to take their wives away and go home; the camels and bulls and horses were led forth, also the wives. And then broke out a quarrel. One of the guests had stolen a silver button off the coat of another man's wife, had cut it off with the scissors as a keepsake, and she had countenanced the theft. The wife, being the personal property of the husband, had, of course, no power to give the button on her own account. There was likely to be an outrageous fight with cudgels, but Liamin appeared in the midst of the dispute and calmed it all away in the name of law and order. The guests mounted and rode away, out into the darkness, by various tracks, on horses, camels, bulls, their wives with them. It was astonishing to see the effect of the appearance of an officer among the angry crowd. They forgot their differences at one look and the recognition of a uniform. Even the dogs ceased barking when they saw the sword of my friend and they smelt his khaki trousers.

Our horses had been taken out of the shafts and given three hours' rest and plenty of oats to eat. We walked out over the wild and empty moor together and chatted, came back and had tea, and then got into the *tarantass* once more. It was the depth of night before we moved on, and although we had clambered in before the horses were brought back, our object being to go to sleep before we started, we went on comparing impressions. I told him my life, he told me his, told me about his wife and children and his home at Przhevalsk, of his horses and his experiments in breeding, of the horse races at Verney, of the joy of the Kirghiz in racing, the one Russian pursuit and interest in which they fully share, the common ground of the two peoples in the colony. Liamin spent a great deal of the year in China and on the frontier, and had evidently much experience of the Chinese. He considered there would be a quarrel with China sooner or later through the progress of Russia in Central Asia. But the Chinese would be beaten. He did not fear their millions. They were not equipped as the Japanese were.

"What do you think of the Yellow Peril; is it getting nearer?" I asked.

"There is no danger of it whatever," said he. "Europe is far too warlike to be in any danger from the Chinese."

"Do you think Europe is more or less warlike than it was; do you think it is getting less warlike?" I asked. This was, of course, before the Great War.

"Yes, it's getting less warlike, I suppose," said Liamin. "But it will be a long while before we are too effeminate to withstand the Mongols. But woe for us if there should ever come such a time! They are a devilish people. At first glance they seem artless and childlike, but you can never be sure what they are up to; they are secret and mysterious. It is an axiom with me that all Asiatics lie; but the Chinese particularly. You remember when San Francisco was destroyed by earthquake the Americans discovered a hitherto unknown and underground city run by the Chinese, and in it many white people who had long since disappeared nobody knew whither, people who had been advertised for and sought for by relatives and police and what not. Wherever the Chinese form colonies they turn to devilry of one kind or another. I remember the ghastly things the Chinese did in the Boxer insurrection, the originality of the tortures they invented. Fancy this as a torture! A Russian whom I knew fell into their hands, and their way of killing him was to fasten a corpse of a man to him, and day and night he lived with this corpse till the worms ate into him and he died of madness! The Russian villagers don't mind doing business with the Chinamen, but always remember they are pagans, and many think they have direct dealings with devils. I was at Blagoveshtchensk when the Chinese opened fire on us, and our Siberian colonists drove all the Chinese out of the city, thirty thousand of them, and they were drowned in the river like rats."

By this time the horses had been put in, Karachok left, and we were jogging gently through the night. The Kirghiz who drove slept; the horses also almost slept as they walked. Liamin at last, tired or made drowsy by the movement, nodded as he talked, and fell asleep in the middle of a sentence. The road climbed over high mountains, the moon bathed the track and the wild and empty landscape with light. How far on either hand stretched the uninhabited world! It was like posting across a new and habitable planet where men might have been expected to be living, but where all had died, or none but ourselves had ever come. The world itself poked up, its great back was shyly lifted as if it were some gigantic, timid animal that had never been disturbed. It was a wonderful night; quiet, gentle, and unusual. Liamin, at my side, slept silently and intensely. The Kirghiz looked as if cut out of wood. I lay back and looked out, my fingers locked behind my head. So the small hours passed. Night seemed to move over us and be left behind, and I saw ahead the creeping dawn, the morrow, the real morrow, golden and lucent on the eastern horizon. The sun rose and flooded into our sleepy and sleeping eyes as we clattered over the brow of a hill. We came to the Tartar hamlet of Kuan-Kuza, and it was morning.

XI

ON THE CHINESE FRONTIER

AT Kuan-Kuza I parted company with Liamin. I went off for a walk on the hills; he went on with Vaska and Margarita. I had now reached mountainous country and a region of fresh air. There were green valleys and wild flowers, streams beside which I could make a pleasant repast, and I had a most enjoyable walk to Kopal. There were patches of snow on the heights, and I clambered up and fingered it just for the joy of realising the contrast to the heat of the deserts I had come through. The road went high over a green tableland to Altin-Emel, where I came to cross-roads for China. An enormous caravan of camels blocked all the ways here; two or three hundred ranks of camels, roped three in a rank, roped crossways and lengthways, bearing huge panniers of wool, but no passengers. Chinamen and little Chinese boys were in charge of them, and ran among the camels' legs cursing and calling as the strings of bewildered or purposely contrary animals threatened to get into knots and inextricable tangles. Sarts were doing a good business here, selling hot lunch from wooden cauldrons with three compartments, in which were meat pies, soups, potatoes, respectively, all cooking at the same time over charcoal. Altin-Emel is an interesting point on the road. Here may be seen upon occasion British sportsmen with Hindu servants, and two or three britchkas full of trophies and large antlers done up in linen and cotton-wool and fixed with rope. Before the war four or five British officers passed through Altin-Emel every year on their way to Chinese Tartary or India, or from those places, coming home. Some were out here at the time the war broke out, and were a long time in finding out exactly what had happened in Europe.

It is very beautiful country, with snow peaks in view in the distance and at your feet white iris, forget-me-not, and brilliant Scotch roses, those yellow blossoms thick on thorny stems. Then there are fields of mullein as thick as stalks of corn after the peasants' sickles have cut the harvest. There are good-looking and frequent Russian villages and Cossack stations, Kugalinskaya, Polovinka, Kruglenkoe. I passed through a village started only in 1911, very clean, well kept, and promising. Kugalinskaya Stanitsa was an old settlement, the land probably given to the Cossacks when the conquest took place. This place was very drunken the time I stayed there, though now, since the war and prohibition, that characteristic must have vanished. The Cossacks apparently found life rather boring; they had a marionette show in the bazaar, lotto banks and roulette tables, where copecks were risked and bottles of vodka staked. The public-house was full of singing drunkards. I can imagine how cheered up the people were when war was declared.

After a wonderful night on a little green tableland covered with mulleins, where when I spread my bed I must crush mulleins, I went on to Tsaritsinskaya. There, on the pass over the mountains and the Kok-sa River, I got my first soaking on this vagabondage, soaked to the skin by mist and drizzle; but I did not seem much the worse for it, and dried naturally in the sun on the morrow, visibly steaming. It was quite like a Caucasus road now, steep, wild, magnificent with gorges and passes, foaming rivulets, villages threaded with the life of running water, the paradise of ducks and their broods. The outward roads were marked by heaps of mud and stones, and on these I went to Jangiz-Agatch, with its fine trees, and Karabulak and Gavrilovka; finally, a day over great sweeps of country illumined by gorse in bloom and yellow roses, over leagues of wolf-hunted moorland to Kopal.

Kopal is 825 miles from a railway station, and one of the last places on earth; a town without an inn, without a barber; a place you could run round in a quarter of an hour, and yet having jurisdiction over an immense tract of territory along the Russian frontier of China. It was late in the evening when I arrived there, and when I went to the post-house I found it crowded with Chinamen; Chinamen on the two beds, on the floor, in the passage; chopsticks on the table. They were all travellers on the road to Pekin, making their way slowly northward to the Trans-Siberian Railway.

At once one of those who occupied a bed got up, apologised, and vacated his sleeping-place, offering it to me. Despite my refusal, he took off his blanket and quilt and spread them on the floor instead. His humility was touching—especially in contrast to my own instinctive loathing of a bed on which Chinese had lain. Fortunately, I did not feel tired.

I do not carry a watch on my travels, so the idea of what time it is gradually fades from the mind. The hour is not a matter of anxiety; dawn, noon, sunset, night are the quarters of the clock, and they suffice. But in the post-station at Kopal, whilst the Chinese were officiously effacing themselves, I found myself idly looking at the big clock hanging in a shadowy corner and trying to make out the hour. The face of the clock was a tiger looking at a snake. When it was twelve o'clock the hands were between the tiger's eyes. At a quarter-past seven the hands held the serpent. The clock was very dusty, but imagine the start I got when suddenly I saw that the eyes in the tiger face were rolling at me. As I stared the pupils slowly moved across the whites of the eyes. The pendulum made the eyes roll.

It was only nine o'clock, and I had noticed as I came into the town a considerable flare of lights, a large white tent, and a notice of a Chinese circus. A Chinese circus was something not to be missed in this empty and outlandish country, so I put down my pack in the post-house and went out to see the performance. It was something truly original, a piquant diversion after a long day's journeying in the wastes and wilds of the mountains of Alai Tau.

It was a circular tent, small enough for a circus tent, having only three rows of seats around the arena. The price to sit down was thirty copecks, to stand behind, fifteen copecks. Soldiers came in free, and there were some thirty of them, with their dull peasant faces and dusty khaki uniforms. Near the entrance there was a box covered with red bunting, free for the chief of police and his friends. The chief of police has a free box at nearly every local entertainment in Russia—he can permit or forbid the show. There were three musicians—Russian peasants, paid a shilling a night, I understand—and they gave value for money unceasingly on a concertina, a violin, and a balalaika. The public on the bare, rickety forms ringed round the as yet empty stage numbered from 100 to 120, and were a mixture of Russians, Tartars, and Kirghiz. All the Russian officers and officials of the town seemed to be there, and were accompanied by their smartly dressed wives and daughters. The Tartar merchants looked grim in their black skull-caps, their women queenly, with little crowns on the tops of their heads and long veils falling over their hair and their backs. There was a row of these crowned Tartar women together; a row also of Kirghiz women, in high, white turbans wrapped about their broad brows. There were colonists and their *babas*—open-faced, simple-souled peasant women who came to be petrified by the seeming devilry of the heathen Chinee. To them the fact that the Chinese are heathen—not Christian—is no joke, but a fierce reality. They look upon the Chinese as being comparatively near akin to devils.

Naphtha lamps swung uneasily from the high beams of the tent, and flung unequal volumes of light from dangerous-looking ragged flames. The sandy arena and all the eager people round were brightly shown in the plenitude of light.

The first item on the programme was not particularly striking. A bell was rung, and a little Chinaman in black came out and twirled and juggled a tea-tray on a chopstick. Then followed a Russian clown with painted face, old hat, and yellow wig, who proceeded to be very serious and show the public various tricks. He had three Chinese servants, and the fun consisted in their stealing his things and spoiling his efforts. Finally, he took a big stick and chased them round and round the arena—to the great delight of all the children present.

The clown's turn ended, there came forward a very handsome Chinee in black satin knee-breeches, tight stockings, scarlet jersey, and English collar and tie. He was rather tall, had a big, womanish face, gleaming teeth, and long, black hair. He walked jauntily in little slippers, and carried a handful of ten knives. Another Chinaman came out with an old tree trunk, which he held up on end. A child came and stood up against the trunk. The handsome

CHINESE PRAYING-HOUSE AT DJARKENT

Chinee then stood and flung the knives as if to pin the boy to the wood, and he planted them between the child's arm and his body, over his arm, between his legs and beside his legs, on each side of his neck, on each side of his ears, and over his head—and all the time as he flung them he smiled. He repeated his feat, placing all the knives round about the boy's head, never raising the skin.

Number four was the owner of the troupe, an old fellow in a light blue, voluminous smock and long pigtail. He conjured a platter of biscuits and cakes, glasses, a teapot, a steaming samovar, all out of nothingness, inviting the public to come and have tea with him, and talking an amusing broken Russian:

"You laugh, you think this fine trick, but I show you 'nother mighty juggle; took me ten years to learn this juggle . . ." and so on.

As the applause dies down the bell rings again, and out comes the "Chinaman with the cast-iron head." All the time "the orchestra" plays Russian dances, plays them very noisily. He with the iron head lies down on the sand and puts two bricks on his temple. At a distance of ten yards another Chinaman holds a brick and prepares to aim it at the head of his prostrate fellow-player. He aims it, but the iron-headed one pretends to lose his nerve and jumps up with a terrible scream, pointing to the music. The music must be calmed down. The audience holds its breath as the trick is repeated to gentle lullaby airs. This time the prostrate man receives the bricks one by one as they are aimed—square on the bricks lying on his temple—and, of course, is none the worse, though he takes the risk of a bad shot.

The old conjurer came out again and danced to the Russian Kamarinsky air, holding a bamboo as if it were his partner, and doing all manner of clever and amusing turns. The young man who juggled the tea-tray on the chopstick reappeared, and did a difficult balancing trick, raising himself on a trestle which rested on little spheres on a table. Then came two most original items, the dancing of an old man in a five-yard linen whip, and the rolling round the body of a rusty eight-foot iron sceptre.

The man who danced made the long whip of linen crack and roll out over the arena in splendid circles and waves, and he was ever in the midst of it. The juggler of the sceptre contrived to roll the strange-looking implement all over his body, about his back and his shoulders and his stomach, and never let it touch the ground and never touched it with his hand—and at the same time to dance to the music. This was a most attractive feat, and was as pleasant to watch as anything I had ever seen in a large city.

There was an interval and a great buzz of talking and surmise. After the interval came wrestling matches and trick-riding on bicycles. A clever little Mongol had no difficulty in disposing of those who offered to wrestle with him, and a Russian cyclist who rode on his handle-bars received great applause

LEPERS IN A FRONTIER TOWN

from the people of Kopal, most of whom had not seen a bicycle before.

So the entertainment ended, and everyone was well pleased. The juggling was a great mystification to the simple Russians, and I heard many amusing comments from those behind me and beside. The conjuring forth of the steaming samovar was especially troubling to the minds of the peasant women, and I heard one say to another:

"God knows where he got it from."

And the other replied seriously:

"What has God got to do with it? It's the power o' Satan."

I returned to my post-house in a pleasant frame of mind; it was one by the clock with the tiger face, and I took out my sheets and blanket and slept in a wagon in the yard. All the Chinese were snoring.

I said Kopal had no barber, but next day I found a Sart who shaved. I entered a dwelling in the bazaar, half home, half cave. Picture me sitting on a rag of carpet on the floor of a mud hut, a red handkerchief tied tightly round my neck. A bald-headed old Mohammedan holds in his hand a broken mug containing vinegar. He dips his thumb in the vinegar, and then massages my cheeks and chin and neck. It was queer to feel his broad thumb pounding against my skin and chinbone. He made no lather, but he thought that he softened my skin with his hard thumb and the vinegar. Then he brandished a broken razor over my head, and fairly tore the hair off my face with it. He gave me no water with which to rinse, but as he finished his job he put into my hand three inches of broken mirror so that I could survey my new countenance and judge whether he had done well.

The Chinese at the post-house behaved like Christians, or, rather, as Christians should, with great humbleness and altruism, giving up the samovar to Russian visitors, fetching water to fill the washing-bowls, cleaning and drying the dishes after their breakfast, and sweeping the post-room floor before they went away. The postmaster's wife said there was a constant flow of Chinese, and they always behaved in that way.

Kopal, four thousand feet above the sea level, is in the midst of fine scenery, and the frontier all the way to Chugachak and the shoulder of the Altai mountains is wild and desolate. The boundary is marked by numbered poles, but there are few soldiers or excisemen to question you if you cross either way. There is a certain amount of smuggling done, one of the articles brought through from China being Havana cigars, of which the local bureaucracy is said to be fond.

Sportsmen on the road to Kuldja sometimes put up at Kopal. They are given facilities to make such journeys and receive honourable treatment, their names being forwarded to all the postmasters on the way and instructions being posted in all the post-houses along the road. It was interesting to read on the post-house walls notices of the following type:

"There will pass this way" (then would come an English name). "You are to give him horses and all of which he may stand in need. In the case of his being hindered for any reason, you will be severely punished."

These English often possess their own *tarantasses*, and sleep in them at night. In that way they avoid the unpleasantness of sleeping in a room full of Chinese. On the whole it is better to sleep out of doors than in.

XII

"MIDSUMMER NIGHT AMONG THE TENT-DWELLERS"

I WALKED forth from Kopal on a broad moorland road, and after several hours' upland tramping came to the Cossack village of Arazan—a typical willow-shaded settlement with irrigation streamlets rushing along the channels between the roadway and the cottages. Here, at the house of a herculean old soldier, I was offered for dinner a dish of hot milk, ten lightly boiled eggs, and a hunch of black bread—the typical meal of the day for a wanderer in these parts. In the pleasant coolness of five o'clock sunshine I passed out at the other end of the only street of the village and climbed up into the hills beyond. I turned a neck in the mountains, descended by little green gorges into strange valleys, and climbed out of them to high ridges and cold, windswept heights. All about me grew desolate and rugged. It was touching to look back at the little collection of homes that I had left—the compact, little island of trees in the ocean of moorland below me and behind me—and look forward to the pass where all seemed dreadful and forbidding in front.

In such a view I spread my bed and slept. The hill-side was covered with mullein stalks, and as it grew dark these stalks seemed to grow taller and taller and blacker all about me till they looked like a great wood of telegraph poles. The vast dark masses of the mountains dreamed, and in the lightly clouded heaven stars peeped across the world, rain-laden winds blew over me, and I had as lief it rained as not, so dry was everything after weeks of summer heat. But no rain came, though the winds were cool and the night was sweet.

Next morning, with great difficulty, I collected roots and withered grass enough to boil a pot and make my morning tea, and I sat and ate my breakfast in the presence of Mrs. Stonechat and her four fluffy little youngsters, gurgling and chirping and not afraid to sit on the same bank with me, while their mother harangued them on "How to fly." While sitting there the large raindrops came at last, and they made deep black spots in the dust of the road, the lightning flashed across my knife, the thunder rolled boulders about the mountains, and I sped to a cave to avoid a drenching shower.

I was in a somewhat celebrated district. The Pass and the Gorge of Abakum are among the sights of Seven Rivers Land, and are visited by Russian holiday-makers and picnickers. All the rocks are scrawled with the names of bygone visitors, and by that fact alone you know the place has a name and is accounted beautiful. When the rain ceased, and I ventured out of the cave again, I saw a Russian at work writing his name. He had a stick dipped in the compound with which the axles of his cart-wheels were oiled, and the wheels of the cart were nearly off for him to get it. For the first time I saw how these intensely black scrawls of names and signatures are written on the rocks. We are content to scratch our names with a bit of glass or a nail, or to chalk them, or cut them with a pocket-knife; but the Russians are fond of bold, black signatures two or three feet long, and they make them with this pitch and oil from the wheels of their carts.

It was a pleasant noontide on the narrow road, between crumbling indigo rocks and heaped debris. The stony slopes were rain-washed, the air fresh, and all along the way these dwarf rose bushes which I had seen on the road to Kopal, thorny, but covered with scores of bright yellow blossoms on little red stems. The jagged highway climbed again high up —to the sky, and gave me a vision of a new land, the vast dead plain of Northern Semi-retchie and of Southern Siberia. Northward to the horizon lay deserts, salt marshes, and vast lakes with uninhabited shores, withered moors and wilted lowlands. I saw at a glance how uninteresting my road was to become if I persevered straight ahead towards Semi-palatinsk, and I resolved to keep to the mountains in which I found myself, and follow them eastward and north-eastward to the remoter town of Lepsinsk.

From that height, which was evidently the famous pass, I descended into the pretty gorge of Abakum. The road was steep and narrow, the cliffs on each side sheer. A little foaming stream runs down from the cliffs, over rubbish heaps of rocks,

A PATRIARCHAL KIRGHIZ FAMILY

and accompanies the highway in an artificially devised channel. A strange gateway has been formed in a thin partition of rock, and through this runs the stream below and the telegraph wire overhead; there is a footway, but carts are obliged to make a detour. At this gateway and on the rocks I saw a further intimation of commercial Siberia. Commercial travellers had scrawled:

BUY PROVODNIK GALOSHES AT OMSK

and

BUY INDIAN TEA AND GET RICH

which was almost as if I had seen in the midst of the wilderness something like "Owbridge's Lung Tonic: 4,000 miles to London." Still, these advertisements of galoshes and tea were scrawled, not printed, and were done voluntarily by enthusiastic travellers who probably received no fee for doing such a thing. In England you cut your Rosalind's name on the tree; in Russia your own name; in America you write what O. Henry called "your especial line of graft," and all the New World is scrawled with hand-written advertisements of trade. So in the far-off gorge of Abakum I saw a suggestion of the America of the future—great commercial Siberia, to which perchance, some day, Americans will emigrate for work as the Russians emigrate to America to-day.

I felt this pass and gateway to be the entrance to Siberia, though, politically, the frontier is about three hundred miles distant. After six or seven turns the road issued forth upon a level strand of green and grey—the Siberian southern steppe. Lepsinsk, my next point, was the first town with a name ending in "sk," and there are scarcely more than four towns in Siberia not ending so. None of the emigrant carts that I now met were coming from the south, but all from Siberia, and many of the emigrants were Siberians discontented with their northern holdings. They seemed poor people, and the caravans were rather woebegone. There is a good deal of land offered to the emigrants in the neighbourhood of Lepsinsk, most of it contiguous to the Chinese boundary; but, though it is green and fertile, it is as hard a land to settle as the plains in the south. The Siberians missed the pine forests, the shelter and the fuel of them, and it was a sight to see the straggling procession of women behind the dust-covered wagons—they had to spread themselves about the moor and the roadway, and search for roots and splinters of wood with which to make a fire at the end of their day's journey. All the women held their aprons or petticoats up, and gathered the fuel into their laps. It took them nearly all day to get enough for the fires to boil the nightly soup.

For me, however, it was a green and joyous road from Abakum eastward to Sarkand, keeping to the mountain slopes and not faring forth upon the scorched plain that lies away northward. I did not repent that the cross-roads tempted me to go eastward, hugging the mountains. Long green grass waved on each side of the road, and in the grass blue larkspur and immense yellow hollyhocks. I was in the land where the Kirghiz has his summer pasture, and often I came upon whole clans that had just pitched their tents. It was a many-coloured picture of camels, bulls and horses, of sheep swarming among children, of kittens playing with one another's tails, of tents whose framework only was as yet put up, of heaps of felt and carpet on the grass, of old wooden chests and antediluvian pots and jugs of sagging leather lying promiscuously together, while the new home was not made. On this road the Chinese jugglers overtook me and camped very near where I slept one night. I was amused to see the old conjurer who had juggled the steaming samovar out of thin air hunting mournfully for bits of wood and roots to make that same samovar boil in real earnest.

Next day I came to the village of Jaiman Terekti and its remarkable scenery. The River Baskau flows between extraordinary banks, great bare rocks, all squared and architectural in appearance, giving the impression of immense ancient fortresses over the stream. These squared and shelved rocks are characteristic of the country-side and the geological formations, and they give much grandeur to what otherwise were quiet corners. The gateway of Abakum itself owes its impressiveness to this geological rune.

At a village hereabout I fell in with four boys going up into the mountains to study for the summer. They were students from some large engineering college, and, as part of their training, they had been sent out to study irrigation works and bridges in this colony. At every bridge we came to on the road they stopped and gave it their consideration, and made notes as to its structure and its necessities, and at each village they considered the control of the mountain streams, the canalisation of the water, and the uses to which the natural supplies of water could be put. They called themselves *hydrotechnics*, and would eventually blossom, perhaps, into irrigation engineers. Their trip was costing them no more than one hundred roubles—say, ten pounds each for the three months of summer. Their head-quarters was to be a village on a river about a hundred miles north of Lepsinsk; there they would pitch their tents and camp, cooking their meals, arranging expeditions, and making good their study. Altogether about three dozen young students would turn up at their camping-ground, and make up the equivalent of a summer class.

The four young men had in their protection a lady in cotton trousers, a tall young woman of athletic appearance and good looks. She and her two little children were on their way to the husband, a Government engineer, who had charge of the building of the new town of Lepsinsk—the nearest railway point to Old Lepsinsk. She was a very striking figure in her *sharivari*, and the natives collected round her and stared in an absurd fashion. She told me she had bought the print for 1 rouble 87 copecks, and made them herself just before starting out; skirts were so inconvenient for travelling in and collected the dirt so. But she drew thereby an enormous amount of attention to herself, it must be said. She was rather a crazy Kate. It tickled me to think how her husband would pitch into her when she arrived at her destination. But perhaps I was mistaken, and he was so homesick that he would not even laugh when she appeared. She was a regular scapegrace, with light blue, torn, openwork stockings, and button boots, one of which was fastened with a safety-pin, the other with two shirt-buttons. But she was very naïve and had bunches of smiles on her lips—the sort to which much is forgiven. When she tried to smack her children, they went for her tooth and nail, and the little boy, aged two, continually imitated someone, probably the father, and addressed his mother thus:

"*Akh tee somnoi ne zagovarivaisia*" ("Don't stand there talking to me."

"*Bross!*" ("Stop it!")

"*Pliun!*" ("Spit!")

I was called upon to imitate cats and dogs and sheep and pigeons and camels, and make-believe generally to an unlimited extent.

The lady told an amusing story of a banquet to which the Kirghiz had invited her husband and herself. It should be explained that the Russian for the head of an animal is *golovo*, and for the head of an expedition or band of workmen is *glavny*, the adjective derived from *golovo*, a head. At this banquet in the Kirghiz tent the engineer was put in the highest seat, and was told that the dinner was coming. Suddenly a Kirghiz appeared with a roast sheep's head, and carried it to the Russian, saying:

"Please, eat!"

"What's this?" asked the engineer. "The head for me; that won't do at all. I don't want the sheep's head; you must cut me something more tasty."

"No, please," said the Kirghiz. "You are the head man, and you must eat the head."

"That will never do," said the Russian. But they besought him to honour their custom and permit the rest to eat, for until he had started on the head nobody else might begin.

All the engineer's workmen were Kirghiz, for he was working in Kirghiz country, in a district as yet untouched by Russian colonisation. The wife and her babies turned off at a mountain track, and were taken to her husband's camping-ground by a Kirghiz. We were loath to let the woman go, for she had given much gaiety to the road.

Lepsinsk is what the Russians call a *medvezhy ugolok* (a bear's corner), a place where in winter the wolves roam the main street as if they did not distinguish it from their peculiar haunts. It is by post-road 945 miles from Tashkent on the one hand, and 1,040 miles from Omsk on the other—roughly, 1,000 miles from a railway station. It is high up on the mountains on the Mongolian frontier, and lives a life of its own, almost completely unaware of what is happening in Russia and in Europe—a window on to Mongolia, as a local wit has called it.

In the course of the next five years a railway is to be run from Semipalatinsk to Verney, and as Lepsinsk is the largest town on the way, it should in justice pass through it. But Lepsinsk is high. When the news of the projected railway came, the burgesses made a petition to the authorities asking to be informed where exactly the railway would be, and they would remove Lepsinsk thither. Everyone who had any business would transfer his stock. They were informed, and in a year, or a year and a half, Lepsinsk promised to remove itself fifty miles westward. Building operations were in full swing on the new site, land having been allowed by the Government free; and the engineer whose wife we had met was in charge. If the war does not preclude the continuation of the railway construction, Old Lepsinsk will be abandoned.

I spent four days in the town in the company of the young *hydrotechnics*. We were given rooms free at the Zemsky guest-house, and I stayed three nights there before resuming my journey toward the Irtish. The students quickly found and made friends with people in the town. We found a family that came from the same country-side as one of the young men, and spent the whole evening in a big farmhouse, drinking tea, trying musical instruments, and singing Russian choruses. Next day we went to the colonists' information office, made friends with the young man in charge, and went and played *pyramid* with him in the town assembly rooms; several other folk came in, young and old, and joined in the game of billiards till we were a dozen or more. After billiards we all sat down to a crude lunch of boiled and undisguised beef, without vegetables, but with jugs of creamy milk to drink. The conversation went on cards, billiards, the coming Sunday-night dance. Couldn't an orchestra be made up to supplant the usual gramophone to which the people danced on Sunday evenings? Had the cinematograph films come, and that had been so long expected? What would happen if one showed a cinema film backward—wouldn't the story be often more funny?

Sunday morning we spent in the domain of the colonists' information bureau, and interviewed peasants for the manager whilst he was still in bed. What a litter there was everywhere—tea glasses, cigarette boxes, picture post cards, electric lamps, old letters, forms issued by the Government, maps—the same in the bedroom as in the office. There was a typewriter, and I amused myself trying to write English sentences with the Russian type, there being a fair number of letters in the Russian language resembling our own. The people who came for information had various pleas. One was ill, another had quarrelled with her husband. An old man pushed in front of him a rather downcast young woman, and commenced his appeal to us in these words: "I recommend this woman to your mercy. The land which is hers is being stolen away from her." She had fallen out with her husband, and

SHEEP SHEARING OUTSIDE THE TENT HOME

had fled to her father's house. But meanwhile the husband was trying to sell the land or raise money on it—at least, so the father said. But we pointed out to him that that was nonsense; the land was not yet the unqualified property of the husband, and he could not sell it; he could only give it back to the Government, and so on and so on. On Sunday evening we all went to the assembly rooms, and saw Lepsinsk in its Sunday best, talked vociferously in crowds, listened to a gramophone, watched peasant girls and young men dance melancholy waltzes—there was no Russian dancing, but the people were glad to think themselves "European." I made acquaintance with the *ispravnik*, or whoever he was who ruled Lepsinsk, and with the local rich men—a remote, obtuse, provincial set, whose only interest was cards. They were very keen on playing me at *preference*, a complex Russian card game which I have generally thought it worth while not to learn, and I was amused to hear that they would teach me, and what I lost would pay for my lesson. I talked a little about England. They got their daily papers three weeks after issue, as a rule, but they read them as new when they came. Their chief idea of our British activities was that the suffragettes were assassinating, murdering, bombing, expropriating, and they chuckled over the fact that our men were not able to manage the women.

Lepsinsk is an out-of-the-way place, and, as far as the road is concerned, a blind alley among the mountains. I was much exercised to know which way I should go next, and I did not want to retrace my steps to Altin-Emel. The map and my route was another topic of conversation among the worthies of Lepsinsk. Everyone gave me a different account of the roads and the ferries. Eventually I decided to cut across country and take the risk of marshes or rushing water lying in my path—a rash decision, as I might after a day or so be forced to walk back to the town and try some other way; but it turned out to be a perfectly happy decision. On this track I saw more of the Cossacks and of the Kirghiz, two races in striking contrast, and I spent Midsummer Night—always a festival night—under very beautiful and unusual circumstances.

Lepsinsk is a Cossack settlement. All the young men are horsemen, have to serve their term in war, and are liable to military service without any exemption or exception. All Cossack families and Cossack villages are brought up on these terms. The children are taught to get on to horseback and ride as we teach our children to walk. They learn the songs which the regiment sings as it comes up the main street on horseback, bearing the black pikes in their hands. The women, whose children and husbands go to the war, are patient as the mother of Taress Bulba. War is the normal condition of life, and the mere manœuvres are taken so seriously that the opposing parties frequently forget that it is only a friendly test, and do one another serious injury. "The Cossacks get so enraged, and they can't stop themselves when they are called upon to charge the sham enemy," said a Lepsinsk boy to me.

On the Monday morning I said good-bye to the students, and, shouldering my knapsack, set off in a north-westerly direction to find Sergiopol, forded the Lepsa river, and climbed out of the green valley where Lepsinsk lies as in a cup. The mountain-sides were rankly verdant, and the purple labiate was thick as in spring-time. It may be remarked that strawberries were not expected to ripen in Lepsinsk for three weeks, whereas six weeks ago in Tashkent they had been a penny a pound.

I passed over the fresh green hills and panted at the gradient, plunged down through beautiful meadows, slept a night in the Cossack station of Cherkask, lying on some felt and being almost eaten up by mosquitoes in what the soldier host called a garden. In this village I saw a pitiful sight—almost naked Kirghiz women treading wet mud and manure into stuff for fuel blocks. They looked astonishingly bestial and degraded. You could not feel that they had any soul or stood in any way above the animals. Yet as young women they had probably been attractive and pretty in their day, and might even have won the fancy of white men. There was a question whether the wife in *Candida* who soiled her lovely fingers putting kerosene into the lamps was really degraded by dirt, but here was something nearer reality.

I slept on the sand beside Gregoriefsky, and next day went deep into the desert, into a land of snakes, eagles, snipe, and lizards. On the Lepsa shore I saw forests of the gigantic reeds with which the houses and bridges are roofed. Here were leagues of ten-feet rushes that waved boisterously in the wind as in a cinema picture. I was warned here against the boa-constrictor; but the worst I saw were intent-eyed little snakes gliding away from me, scared at the sound of the footfall. I got my noonday meal of koumis in a Kirghiz *yurt*, borrowed a horse with which to get across the difficult fords, one of black, reed-grown mud, the other of swift-flowing water. All day I ploughed through ankle-deep sand, and but for the fact that the sun was obscured by cloud, I should have suffered much from heat. As it was, the dust and sand-laden wind was very trying. Early in the evening I resolved to stop for the day, and found shelter in one of twenty tents all pitched beside one another in a pleasant green pasture-land which lay between two bends of the river—a veritable oasis. Even here, as I sat in the tent, I listened to the constant sifting of the sand on the felt sides and roof.

It was a good resting-place. An old man spread for me carpets and rugs, and bade me sleep, and I lay down for an hour, the sand settling on me all the time, and blowing into my eyes and my ears and my lips. In the meantime tea was made for me from some chips of Mongolian brick tea. The old Kirghiz took a black block of this solidified tea dust and cut it with an old razor. The samovar was an original one. It had no tap, and leaked as fast as it

IN SUMMER PASTURE: EVENING OUTSIDE THE KIRGHIZ TENT

would pour. Consequently, a bowl was set underneath to catch the drip. This filled five or six times before boiling-point was reached, the contents of the bowl being each time returned to the body of the samovar.

After tea I went out and sat on a mound among the cattle, and watched the children drive in sheep and goats and cows, and the wives milk them all. It was a scene of gaiety and beauty. There were many good-looking wives, slender and dainty, though they were so short in stature, had white turbans on their heads and jackboots on their feet. As they went to and fro, laughing among themselves and bending over the cattle, their breasts hanging like large full pears at the holes made in their cotton clothes for the convenience of their babies, they looked a very gentle and innocent creation. These women did all the work of milking, and I saw them handle with rapidity ewes, she-goats, cows, mares, draining all except the last into common receptacles. The mares' milk alone was kept separate, to be made into koumis. I must say my taste rebelled against a mixture of sheep's milk, goats' milk and cows' milk, even when made sour; but the Kirghiz were not worried with such fastidiousness.

When the milking was accomplished fires were lit in oblong holes dug in the earth outside the tents—the Kirghiz stoves. Bits of mutton were cut up and fixed on skewers and placed over the glowing ashes in the holes. So supper was cooked. I was called into a tent, and there made to sit on a high wooden trunk, while eight or ten others sat below me on rugs. "You are a *barin*," said the oldest man. "You must have the highest seat." Seated up there, they brought me about a dozen skewers of grilled mutton on a wooden plate and bade me eat. I should not have been surprised to see a sheep's head brought in to me.

"Oh," I said, "it's far too much for me."

"You eat first," said the old man. "Then we will eat."

So I took a skewer and put them at their ease. There were in the tent the old man, his son, two wives of the latter, several children, an old woman, and a minstrel. Outside and in other tents were many sons-in-law and daughters-in-law and cousins, a whole genealogical tree of a family. Among the Kirghiz all sons remain in the father's and father's father's family; only the girls change families, sold or arranged for in marriage. The men all wore hats, or, rather, bonnets, trimmed with an edging of fox's fur, and the foxes from whose thighs this fur had been taken had been captured by trained eagles. The Kirghiz are deeply versed in falconry, and have diverse birds for various preys: hawks for cranes, for plovers, and for hares. They hunt the fox, whose skin is very precious, with eagles. They carry the hawks on their wrists when they ride, and for the support of heavy birds they have stalls or rests coming up from their saddles to hold the bird arm, whilst they hold the horse's reins with the other. The most interesting man in the tent in which I supped was the minstrel, a tall, gaunt heathen in ragged cotton slops; he thrummed on a two-stringed guitar and improvised Kirghiz songs till the dusk grew dark and midsummer night came out with countless stars over the desert and the tents and the cattle and the wanderers.

Asked whether I would sleep inside the tent or out, I preferred the open air, and my hosts made a couch for me, a pile of rugs over an uneven thickness of mown clover. And there I lay and watched the stars come into their places in the sky as at the lifting of a conductor's baton. It was St. John's Eve, a night of mystery and of remembrances. A young moon looked down on me. In the twenty tents around me were singing and music and momentary strange illuminations. Inside the tents the Kirghiz set fire every now and then to piles of weeds, which flared up, causing all the felt walls and roofs of the tents to glow like strange, enormous, shimmering paper lanterns, like fire reflected in silver. They would suddenly glimmer and glow and glimmer again, the light would go, and the grey-white tent would be opaque again.

All night across the sleeping encampment came volumes of music from young throats, the songs of the children minding the cattle. The stillness of the night reigned about this music, and was intensified by the *dun-dun* of rusty camel-bells, the jangle of the irons on hobbled horses, the occasional sneeze of a sheep with a cold, and the hullabaloo of dogs barking on false alarms. I lay and was nibbled under by goats, trying to get at the clover, and breathed at by ruminating cows.

So the night passed. Orion chased the Pleiades across the sky. The eyes that stared or lay open and were stared at by the stars drooped, and eyelids came down over the little windows. Sprites danced among us, tiptoed where we slept, breathed devilry upon our faces and dusty clothes, and I dreamed sweetly of home and other days.

Next morning I felt the turn of the year and looked forward to the glorious autumn and the new life coming after the long journey and the much tramping.

I was up at the dawning and away before the hot sun rose. The old man of the Kirghiz gave me my breakfast himself, a pot of *airann* and a cake of *lepeshka,* and came forward with me, showing me the track onward towards Sergiopol.

XIII

OVER THE SIBERIAN BORDER

I CROSSED the Lepsa by a bridge made of old herring barrels, struck the highway to Sergiopol at Romanovskaya, and pursued my journey along the sandy wastes and salt swamps on the eastern borders of Lake Balkhash. The Lepsa falls into this great lake at last. The wind blew up the sand so that there was some chance of missing the way, and I sat some hours on my knapsack and shut my eyes to keep the sand out. It was dreary country, yellow and inhospitable. The odour of the bleached grasses and herbs was almost overpowering, and food and palatable water were far to seek. Tall, bleached and withered grasses and white weeds and dust-laden, knobbly steppe; wind and racing sand—sand in my eyes, in my mouth, on my body—I felt a most despicable creature, and questioned my sanity in ever starting out on such an absurd journey as this through Russian Central Asia. But I saw ahead of me Sergiopol, Semipalatinsk, and a happier clime. Sixty versts north of Romanovskaya the road, gradually ascending a long moor, entered broken country through black and rusty mountainettes, and here was a little crooked gorge with a stream through it, and it was possible to sit by my own little fire and make tea for myself once more. Then more moorland, and heavily scented grass, and enormous bustards, the size of goats, and skinny little brown marmots, and withered mullein stalks, and comical blue jackdaws perching on them and cocking their heads to one side and peering at me as I passed. Then streams of colonists and their carts. Then an official and his wife, sleeping in their night attire in their slowly moving *tarantass*, huge pillows for their heads, and sheets and quilts and what not—an example of the Russians' gift for making themselves at home. Near Ince-Agatch I met two Germans going cheerfully along on foot—as I was—a botanist and a geologist, neither of them speaking Russian, but feeling pretty well as much at home as in Germany, more so, perhaps. One wonders what was their fortune at the outbreak of war. There are certain international pursuits that know no restriction of national or imperial ground. I do not suppose the Russian grudges the German making a study of his flowers and rocks—if he is not spying at the same time. Probably we ought not to lay so much stress on purely national research in ornithology, entomology, geology, botany, the ways of peoples, and so forth. Individuals and their work are dedicated to their nation and their empire, but that should not keep our practical scientists, collectors, prospectors, students to a mere portion of the surface of the globe. Russian Central Asia and Siberia claims greater attention from our scientific men, hunters, and expert collectors. Russians, on the

FOUR WIVES OF A RICH KIRGHIZ

whole, do little; Germans have done something; but it does not matter by whom it is explored, there lies here a vast natural field for the study of mankind. These domains are scarcely touched, except by vulgar gold hunters and rock tappers—people of paltry greed and little imagination. The great era of research has not even begun, and libraries of books have yet to be written on the natural wonders and astonishing discoveries to be found and made in this wilder and more neglected half of Asia. After the war Siberia and Russian Central Asia will begin to draw more attention from us.

Sergiopol, the last point in Seven Rivers Land before entering Siberia, is a beautifully situated diminutive town, or, rather, village, for it has been degraded from the rank of town. The hills and moors around it are beautiful virgin country, bathed in pleasant sunshine and breathing healthful air; but in itself it is but a miserable place, a collection of wee grocer-shops and cotton stores. The shopkeepers are mostly Tartars, doing very small trade and thinking it very large and feeling "passing rich." The vendors of cotton goods do the most trade, for all the Kirghiz wear cotton and give a great deal of consideration to the purchase of it. I met a commercial traveller smoking a cigarette in the market-place, a man sent out by one of the great cotton firms of Moscow, and he was carrying bags of samples to all the stores of Seven Rivers Land. The Tartars took so long to decide what they were going to buy that the traveller was reduced to a novel procedure. Directly he arrived at a settlement he took from his chest eight bags of samples, and went rapidly from one shop to another, leaving a bag at each, and saying he would return in an hour and a half. Then he went into the market-place and had a smoke and chat with chance comers. If there were more than eight shops he had a second round, and distributed the bags to the remainder after the first set had come to a decision. Not a very good way of doing business, one would think; but, then, the Tartars spoke in their own language, consulted their wives about materials and colours, and liked to be free of the presence of the Russian. He did quite a good business. He told me that his cotton goods found a large market in China. The Chinese and the Kirghiz were extremely critical as to the quality of the cotton and the colour and design. You could not palm off shoddy cotton on these people. It was their Sunday best as well as week-day, and their outer garment as much and more than under-garment. Its quality and appearance mattered. Neither German cotton nor their own Lodz manufacture was any use. Lodz is the great centre for the production of shoddy cotton—so much so that the adjective Lodzinsky is a Russian colloquialism for shoddy, and when you say *Lodzinsky tovar* it is more than when we say "a bit of Brummagem." Moscow, however, produces good qualities of cotton and good prints. Manchester has dropped behind Moscow in this respect and tended to compete rather with Lodz. Perhaps after the war we shall solve this passion for

AT A KIRGHIZ FUNERAL

cheapness, this competition with Germany in turning out *cheap* wares, and will revert to our earlier prejudice in favour of British quality. It is rather touching in Russia that best quality goods are often called *Anglisky tovar* (English wares), even when made in Russia. Our reputation for thoroughness survives.

Still, I do not suppose that Great Britain will ever compete with Russia in the supply of cotton to the interior. Russians and English living in Russia have imported our British machinery and set up mills which are really British mills on Russian soil, and an enormous business has been founded. Russia, moreover, hopes to be able to grow enough raw cotton in her Central Asian dominions to be able to make her cotton business a national self-dependent industry. Cotton is the material mostly used for clothing in Russia, even in the towns. The women are still content with cotton dresses and the men with cotton blouses. When cloth and "stuff" come in, if they ever do, the cotton industry will tend to degenerate, but not till then.

Sergiopol is a place of little significance. But the next town, Semipalatinsk, in Siberia, is a large colonial town, with over 35,000 inhabitants—larger, even, than Verney. But Siberia is an old-established Russian colony, while Seven Rivers began only fifty years ago, and was a desert. Perhaps even now it is little more than a desert qualified by irrigation. The obstacles in the way of successful settlement have been tremendous. Still, these obstacles are being overcome. The result of half a century's work is a measure of clear success and a healthy promise. Hundreds of Russian villages have established themselves, and the channels of small trade have been kept open. Yellow deserts have become green with verdure, and chains of oases have been made. Russian schools and Russian churches have arisen on the northern side of India, and an essentially Christian culture is spreading in a way that is clearly profitable to the Old World. The colony sadly needs a railway, and the railway is being built quickly, even now, in the time of the war. For the Kirghiz, who do most of the labour, are not required for military service. When the railway comes, more people will come with it, more colonists, more traders, and they will take away the products which the farmers would gladly sell. We are accustomed to think of railways spoiling districts, but Russian Central Asia, with its empty leagues of sand and barrenness, will only profit by the railway. The railway must go east from Tashkent all the way to Verney, and probably as far as Kuldja, in China, then northward, through Iliisk and Sergiopol, to Semipalatinsk, through Siberian farms and settlements, forests and marshes, to the Siberian main line at Omsk. This will greatly strengthen the Russian Empire when it is achieved. It will be a wise measure of consolidation.

M. de Vesselitsky, in his able book on Russia, remarks that whereas in 1906 the population of Canada was greater than that of Siberia, in 1911

Siberia had two million more inhabitants. This is the more astonishing because Canada has splendid and populous towns, whereas Siberia has only three cities of over a hundred thousand inhabitants. A strange contrast to European Russia, this Asiatic Russia; no Court, no Emperor, no artistocracy, no modern aims or claims, no power—in a sense, human tundra and taiga, though many millions are living there. Then a power enters it, commercial capital and the Russian desire to get rich, and Siberia begins to seek new wealth. European Russia and the dazzling if somewhat tawdry West begins to hear of the wealth of Siberia. Our civilisation, the centre of attraction, draws from all the outside wilds and wildernesses gold, precious stones, skins. So we help Siberia in the material sense and set its industrial life a-going.

XIV

ON THE IRTISH

THE most interesting circumstance in the history of Semipalatinsk up till now is that Dostoieffsky, in exile, was domiciled there. The cities dotting the wastes of Siberia are not notable. They are young, and things have not happened in them. But dreary Semipalatinsk held the mightiest spirit in modern Russia—Fedor Dostoieffsky, the author of "The Brothers Karamazof." So Semipalatinsk, on the loose sands of the River Irtish, has now its Dostoieffsky house, where Dostoieffsky lived, and a Dostoieffsky street. It will, no doubt, be a place of pilgrimage in the future for those wishing to grasp the significance of the great Russian.

Semipalatinsk is a dull collection of wooden houses and stores, an important trading centre functionising an immense country-side. What struck me most were the large general shops, with their extensive supplies of manufactured goods and all manner of luxuries. There were at least six department stores, with handsome clocks, vases, bedroom furniture, mandolins, violins, guitars, Vienna boots, American boots, gay hats, silk dresses, wrapped chocolates, promiscuous and lavish supplies of all manner of European goods. English wares seemed noticeable chiefly by their absence, and the cutlery was Swedish, the stoves Austrian, the wools and the cottons Russian, the note-paper American or French, the wonderful enamel ware and nickel and aluminium ware German. Only sanitary contrivances, cream separators, and agricultural machinery seemed to be English. How much more of these things might be sent. However, with all these signs of luxury—luxury for Russians—Semipalatinsk lacks the graces of a town; has no lighting, no pavement or public place, no theatre, only a cinema. Its prospect is waste, loose sand, which the air holds even in calm—a grit in the eyes and in the mouth. Its trees do not flourish, and only people accustomed to a quiet life could go on living there from year to year. The peasants bring most life into the town, selling their products in the immense open market, or buying manufactured goods to take up-country to their farms. The broad River Irtish flows placidly onward, five hundred miles to Omsk and thousands of miles to the Arctic Ocean, and it is navigated by a considerable number of steamers and sailing boats. It is a great waterway—a sort of safer sea in the heart of Asia. The wonder is that more towns have not sprung up on its shores. In the history of the world it has not yet become a typical river. It flows from the silences of the Altai mountains, through the silences of Northern Asia, the noise of man hardly ever becoming more than a whisper upon it. It never becomes

> Bordered by cities and hoarse
> With a thousand cries,

and it cannot be said that as we go onward to its mouth

> Cities will crowd to its edge
> In a blacker incessanter line;
> That the din will be more on its banks,
> Denser the trade on its stream.

It is almost as peaceful and serene as a river in an undiscovered continent.

At Semipalatinsk I stayed some days before taking boat up-stream to Malo-Krasnoyarsk. It was here that I read of the astonishing intelligence of the assassination of the Archduke of Austria and his wife. The Russian papers of the time devoted a great deal of space to the details of the murder, the reprisals taken by the Austrians, the gossip of Europe. The preoccupation of the British Press with home affairs was astonishing, and in all the telegraphed opinions of our representative papers there was not an utterance that overstepped the limits of conventionality. Whether the murder was planned politically by Germany, as has been hinted, or planned politically by Serbia for vengeance, or came about accidentally through the passion of a noble Serb, it was in any case a test phenomenon. It had enormous significance to diplomatists and scanners of political horizons. By the attitude and behaviour of Germany and Austria their intentions, at least in the Near East, could be gauged. But it did not seem of sufficient importance to conscious England. The Austrians tried to spread the idea that Russia had contrived and bought the murder of the Archduke because she feared his intentions in the Balkans. But, out of the Germanic dominions, that did not carry weight. Austria manifestly threatened Serbia politically, and some British people scratched their heads and asked questions: "Shall we go to war for Serbia?" Then came the seemingly obvious answer: "No, not for *Serbia!*" which fairly indicates the blindness of that part of England which was vocal at that time. In that spirit we neglected our duty in connection with the St. James's conference after the first Balkan war, and in that spirit we alienated Bulgaria in the great European war which followed.

Austria threatened war, and there was clearly the prospect of Austria and Russia fighting. I weighed it up in my mind as I waited at Semipalatinsk, and more than once I asked myself whether I had not better give up my journey onward and go straight to Western Russia. But, deciding I did not want to write war correspondence, I concluded I would continue my way, and rest as I had intended—on the verdant Altai. So I left Semipalatinsk and went in a little steamer up the narrowing and rocky river, past wooded islands, grey moors, and emerald marshes. It was a long though not monotonous river journey. We stopped at elementary wooden landing-stages beside small hamlets, bought eggs, fish, fruit from peasant women and children, backed out into midstream again, making our big wave that went washing along the banks and drenching incautious boys and girls; we beat up the water with our paddle, turned, saw ourselves clear of the pier, and a widening stretch of water between us and the bank, found our course between the buoys, avoided the weirs and the shallows. Morning became hot noon, and the afternoon and twilight time came on, and then luminous starry night, and again morning and hot noon. We stopped at the little town of Ust-Kamennygorsk, the headquarters for several mining camps, a bit of qualified civilisation not unknown to British mining engineers. We had on board a couple of priests, a commercial traveller, some workmen coming back from doing a job, and two dozen raw Cossacks who had been ordered to serve on the Chinese frontier—rather interesting to reflect now how they were travelling away from the place where they would be needed. At that time all the preparations for war were going on apace in Germany; the roads were full of horses newly bought by the Government, the trains full of stores; at the military camps the last manœuvres were being worked out with full regiments and the complete panoply of war. We in the steamboat were all travelling the wrong way, away from the interest of the world—the centre—up-stream on the fast-flowing river, against the currents and the tendencies. A month later all would come back, forced by the declaration of war. Still, little we recked. We had a holiday spirit. There were several high-school girls and girl students on board—*gimnasistki* and *kursistki*—and the deck was vocal with their chattering and laughing. They were a charming contrast to rough Siberia. The

KIRGHIZ PRAYING

deck passengers drank vodka and sang. Down below deck was a public stove, and there sizzled a score of pots—pots with jam, with eggs, with fish, with chickens, with milk. I made my coffee there, and would frequently see it rising at the boil and be unable to pick the pot out for others tending their fish-soup and women taking the scum off their strawberry jam. At each little village people bought things to cook, so that at times you might have thought it was a sort of cooking expedition.

So we went on at this momentous time in history. The river became more rapid and difficult to navigate; it serpentined through wild gorges, where the rocks were broken and ragged and squared and angular. The steep cliffs were full of detail that was delicious to the eye. Where the cliffs were not so steep Nature had clothed their nakedness with mould and grass. We passed from placid stretches which seemed to throw the rays of the sun back on the ship, the people and the sky, and we entered the intense cold shadow of high, sheer rocks. The water became green and shadowy. The scenery changed every moment as we went round a new bend of the river and entered new territory through forbidding gates of rock. Frequently we found ourselves in foaming cauldrons from which there seemed to be no exit; we wandered round, travelling as often north as south, and catching glimpses of sun from all imaginable quarters, and found loopholes of escape to new reaches. The steamer seemed a toy beside the huge cliffs on each side, and the sunshine, when we came into it, seemed sufficient to blind the whole Altai. The higher we pursued our winding way the higher became the cliffs, till eventually we had grey crags of several hundred feet hanging over us. In the earlier gorges the greenness of the vegetation of the hills was reflected in the river in a deep, shadowy green, but in the later ones the drear greyness of the cliffs was alone reflected, and the swift-moving, placid water looked like oil. As far as Gusinaya Pristan trees—birches—but infrequent ones, and growing in haphazard ways from clefts in rocks. Besides our panting, puffing steamer, with its streamer of dense smoke and persistent showers of sparks, there were only rafts on the river—logs roped together, and peasants standing on the water-washed floating platforms. They seemed to be very skilful in managing them. On the banks we saw occasional tents and fishermen's tackle, small fires with tripods over them, and old black pots whereby you guessed that fish were cooking. Occasional hay-making parties also visible on the wan outskirts of farms. It was a fascinating journey, and one could not take one's eyes from the changing scene, the prospect from door after door as we passed new rocks, the delicious side views, the clefts and wounds healed with birch trees and greenery, the battered, jaggy prominences, dull blue, purple, yellow with age and many weathers.

Every one watched curiously for the next scene, and the change was so frequent that no one got tired. Mountains, ridges—the grandeur of our rock basins multiplied upon us so that we felt we were steadily ascending a high mountain rangc by river. Night was wonderful, especially when we stopped to put some cargo off or to take on wood, and we got out and walked on the cliffs and the sand; the stars in the sky had their drips of golden reflection in the river, and the opposite banks and rocks were majestically silhouetted against the sky. The navigation of this river is, perhaps, one of the sights of the future. "Parties will be taken out." But there is no romance there, no castles, no ruins—only Nature and the grey tumultuous misery and beauty of a scarred continent.

XV

THE COUNTRY OF THE MARAL

MALO-KRASNOYARSK, on the Irtish, is a hot, sandy village supporting itself by agriculture, fishing, and melon growing. It is treeless, no one seeming to have cared to plant the trees which could so easily have been grown, and the native Kirghiz are employed making fuel blocks out of manure. The stacks of these black blocks give an unpleasant odour when the wind is blowing over them. Otherwise, the Irtish is rather wonderful—deep and green and swift, with powerful currents.

From Malo-Krasnoyarsk I journeyed along the burnt road and over the vast stretches of pungent wormwood that grow on the moors. The road climbed to the mountain ridges of the Narimsky range, and along them to the Central Altai. I had given up tramping now, and an old man in a dirty crimson blouse drove me in a cart to Bozhe-Narimsky village, took me for three shillings, and was ready to drive me to Kosh Agatch, on the other side of the mountains, if I would say but the word. Kosh Agatch, according to his reckoning, would be five hundred miles, and he would have to plan a month's journey over the mountains, hire extra horses, and buy provisions. According to him traders made the journey frequently, especially Tartars and Chinamen, buying maral horns.

On the higher slopes of the Altai the sale of the horns of the maral deer (*Cervus canadensis asiaticus*) seems to be, if not the chief, at least the most picturesque means of earning a livelihood. I was making my way into the maral country. Here the colonists, instead of farming sheep and cows, farm a species of deer with very valuable horns—the maral. The horns are not valuable as ornaments, or as bone, or as drinking vessels, but as medicine. A very curious trade. The Russians cut off the horns of the deer every spring, boil them, dry them, and sell them into China, where they sell at the rate of about a shilling an ounce, and give almost miraculous relief to women in the pains of childbirth, make it possible for barren women to have children, and many other things.

"Is it good for that purpose?" I asked of the man who was driving me.

"They say so," said he, without committing himself.

"But do Russian women use this medicine?"

"No; it's too expensive."

"But do they believe in it?"

"No, they don't need it. They are not like the Kitankas and Mongolians, who suffer very much. These Chinawomen are like the camels here. The camels would die out if it were not for the skill the Kirghiz women have in making them breed. They would die out, but the Kirghiz keep them going. The same with the Chinawomen; they need the powder of the maral horn. No Chinawoman of any importance thinks of marrying without a pair of maral horns in her possession, and if her father be too poor to purchase them, the husband must. They all use it, and you can buy the powder in any chemist's shop in China."

"Or an imitation?" I suggested.

My driver could not say whether the substance could be imitated. Later on, on my journey, I saw marals, both on the run and in the immense maral gardens which the Russians keep in their colony.

Bozhe-Narimsky was a pleasant green corner, with tumbling river, many willow trees, mosquitoes, marshes. Thence the road went higher and higher to Maly Narimsky and Tulovka, through districts where once were forests of great pines and now are only forests of stumps, through wildernesses of pink mallow and purple larkspur, and over vast, swelling uplands covered with verdure, finally to within sight of gleaming streaks of snow and ice, the glaciers of the central range. Bozhe-Narimsky, Maly Narimsky, Tulovka, Medvedka, Altaiskaya, Katun-Karagai were the names of the Russian villages and Cossack stations on the way up. Most of them were well-established settlements, for this territory is Siberia, and not what is called Russian Central Asia. It has been in Russian hands a long while, and only the fact that Russia is so vast, and there is so much room for the overflow of population, explains the backwardness of the colonisation of the Altai. Russia has never had any enemies worth the name here, and has very little to fear unless the Chinese ever turn bellicose. The only people who stood in her way were the mild nomads, the Kalmeeks and the Kirghiz. These had unrecognised rights to certain valleys, springs, winter pastures, summer pastures, and they walled off their discoveries with stones and boulders, never dreaming anyone would think of annexing them. But when the Russian generals came riding down the valleys with their engineers, saying, "Fix me a village here and a village there, and give us twenty villages along the length of that valley," no Kirghiz or Kalmeek had the spirit to say nay, and with a melancholy smile they crept away, leaving the fields to those who must take them.

Near Tulovka I saw the first marals, six speedy deer running ahead of as many horsemen, just outrunning their horses, but not disposed to race out of sight and get lost. The horsemen, who were Cossacks, carried lassos in their hands, and I rather wondered why they did not shoot the deer and have done with their hunting. A villager put me right, however.

"These are not wild deer, but escaped ones," said he. "There are no wild deer left; they have all been caught now. No one has seen a wild maral for fifteen years. They have all been caught and put in gardens, and now we breed them. If they shoot these marals they lose six good breeders. A buck maral is worth two hundred roubles. It's a sad day for the man who has lost these. It is very difficult to catch them, they are very crafty; and then one doesn't want to injure their horns in taking them. They generally have to ride them down until they are dead beat; no use frightening them; just keep them on the move and give them no rest."

At Medvedka I stayed with an old man who kept a maral farm. My host was a comical fellow, somewhat over six feet high, with long hair, bushy beard, kind and gentle eyes—a giant's shoulders, an ogre's stomach, but the walk and manners of a child. His great pine log house had a threshold so large that you might almost call it a veranda but that peasants do not have verandas. There were steps up to it, and then a long covered way, one side of which was the log wall of the house, in which peeped wee glass windows; the other side was a solid little railing, where you could lean and watch the pigs, the turkeys, the geese, the horses and dogs in the big farm-bounded farmyard. Beyond the yard and the pasture stretched upward the voluminous and irregular mountain-side, deep in a tangle of shadowy undergrowth and made majestical by mighty firs. The gloom and splendour of the mountains brooded over the big log house.

On the veranda were a whole series of green, many-branching antlers just sawn away from heads of marals—an unusual sight in any cottage. They were velvety and hairy; if you touched them you found them soft. Not the antlers hunters bring home and hang on their walls, nothing hard or sharp or fearsome, but gentle, rounded and smooth-knobbed, un-

IN THE ALTAI: KIRGHIZ TOMBS NEAR MEDVEDKA

ripened antlers, sawn off from a stag's head with a saw.

Mikhail Nikanorovitch, mine host, took me up to his maral farm, a tract of mountain-side many acres in extent, fenced in by a gigantic paling, the posts of which were eight or nine feet high and very solid. The maral is a magnificent jumper, and has been known to clear eight feet upon occasion and get away. As the farmer has to buy the posts from the Government, the construction of a *maralnik*, as they call it, is not without considerable expense for the peasants. Quite a small place would cost two hundred roubles.

Mikhail and I stumped up the mountain-side quite a height till we came to his wild enclosure. Mine host called the deer as his peasant wife might have called chickens to their food, and they came fluttering towards him to be fed, but, spying me, stopped short, sniffed the air, then turned and fled to the wildernesses of their prison.

"In the summer they are in this big place," said Mikhail, "but in late autumn, before the snows, we drive them into a smaller place, and we feed them there all the winter. It is in this smaller place that we saw off the horns in the early summer."

He took me along to the shed where the horns were sawn off.

"We make the first cutting only when the calf has reached its third year. We cut off the horns in June and the beginning of July—when the antlers are most developed and so worth most. If we leave them later they harden and are no use. They would then have to be allowed to bear their horns till next spring, when in any case they shed them."

"What happens to those who have had their antlers sawn off; do they shed the stumps?" I asked.

"Yes, they shed their stumps. That is in April or May; and then they change their coats and are generally in a bad state of health."

He described how they managed the animal during the sawing business: put its fore-legs in a noose, its hind-legs in a noose, threw it on the ground, bandaged the eyes, someone carefully holding the head and saving the horns from damage all the time. They sawed off the horn with an ordinary hand-saw—such a one was lying on a sort of bench in the shed to which the old fellow had led me—and when the sawing was done they stopped the bleeding with coaldust and salt, and then tied up the stump tightly with linen. The blood soon stops flowing, and the maral, being put at liberty, forgets and scarce knows what he has lost. In their tamed state the deer have found a sort of alternative destiny, and the peasants say that often marals which escape in the summer come back voluntarily to the enclosures for food and shelter in winter-time. Still, some do finally disappear, and although the villager I met earlier was of opinion that all the marals had been caught, there must still be many thousands at large upon the vast and unexplored Altai. In their wild state they are extremely shy of human beings, and seemingly with good reason.

The Boiling of the Horns

Old Mikhail, who was a kind of three-storied man, pottered about, stooping the whole length of his huge body to pick wild strawberries and raspberries, and he constantly called out to me to help myself to fruit. When we got back to the farmhouse I found his wife boiling a chicken for me in a pail over a bonfire in the garden.

Mikhail showed me where they boiled the horns, and explained the process of preservation. There were enormous coppers for the boiling. The horns were put into boiling brine, just dipped in and taken out several times. The difficulty was to immerse them and yet not touch the metal sides of the pots. If the sides were touched the delicate skin might easily be frayed. After the immersion the horns were exposed in the open air. They dried fairly rapidly, and lost weight; by the time they would be ready for sale they would have lost half their original weight. In the late summer and autumn Chinese and Tartar merchants appeared and made great deals in maral horns throughout the whole district. In China the substance of the horn is known as *ludzon*.

Mikhail was an extraordinarily hospitable type of peasant, and heaped plenty on the table that evening—a great crust of honeycomb, for he kept his own bees and possessed a hillside dotted with white hives; wooden basins full of berries; butter—and butter is rare enough in peasants' houses; and soup and chicken and white bannocks. We had an amusing talk about England. He had never seen a train, the sea, an Englishman, or a German or a Frenchman, or, indeed, any race but Russian, Kirghiz, Chinamen, Tartars, Kalmeeks. We compared the prices of things, and he was greatly alarmed at the cost of meat in England. I made him wonder more and more.

"Now, for instance, a hare," said I. "I do not suppose they cost much here, but in our country we pay six or seven shillings for one at Christmas."

Mikhail was astonished.

"What, for the skin?" asked he.

"Oh, no; we don't value the skin—throw it away or sell it to the rag-and-bone man for twopence."

"You don't mean to say you pay that for a hare. Now, here we keep the skin to sell and throw away the flesh. It's good enough for hogs. I never thought of a hare having a price as food. I don't know that I could say what was the price of hare's flesh here. We throw it away."

He played with the idea, and then eventually inquired of me whether it were possible to get an iced freight-truck from Omsk to London, and what would it cost.

I could not say.

"Well," said Mikhail, "supposing we put a nominal price of two copecks (a halfpenny) a hare exported from here, we could make a big profit, and it seems to me they could be got to London, and there would be a big profit for every one concerned."

I promised to give the matter my consideration, and he was so much in earnest that, despite the fact he had never seen a train and could neither read nor write, he made me note his address carefully and take it to England, where I could give it to a *commersant*, and he would contrive matters.

"Tell him," said he, "that we can let him have ten hares for a rouble. Good night."

I was getting ready to lie down. Some overcoats had been spread on the floor for me.

"Tell him there's no end to the number of hares to be had here. Good night," said he again.

And after I had lain down he came to me again and said:

"Are you comfortable? There was a man here once who made his fortune exporting *sarka* skins. Good night."

Next morning he gave me a large metal pot of honey and black currants mixed, as a present, and he drove me to Altaiskaya Stanista, the top of the Altai, himself.

XVI

THE DECLARATION OF WAR

IT is a fine mountain road from Medvedka to Altaiskaya, over mighty open upland where the great firs grasp the earth with talon-like roots. Here and there along the road are Kirghiz tombs enclosed by rude hurdles, reminding one of the palings of the maral gardens. An occasional Russian hut, a mountain stream pouring across a road, forests of stumps, and again forests of those giant firs standing as against the wind—storm trees, broad at base, needle-pointed at the apex, every branch a strong son.

At Altaisky I proposed to stay a few weeks, and then cross the mountains to the Kosh Agatch road, northward toward Biisk; but the tidings of war came across my plan here, and farther than the Altai I did not go. But I had a quiet fortnight in a wonderful spot—Altaiskaya, opposite Mount Belukha, one of the great snow peaks that stand on sentry here between China and Siberia, and I walked and climbed. It would be a splendid place in which to spend a whole summer. There are places that are so placid and beautiful that you exclaim: "Good heavens, this is a very paradise!" When you have been there a day you want to stay there for ever, or to go away and to return and return again. So it was at little Bobrovo on the Dwina, so again at Altaisky. I thought to myself I shall come here again and spend six months, and write a long and interesting story. And I will ask "Pan" to come, and he also will come and write a wonderful story. "Pan" is an English friend, a great, tall, gentle, quick-scented human, a dear mortal who snuffs the air with his nose and can tell you thereby what has happened in a place any time this three weeks past.

Altaiskaya was full of the freshness of youth, and the air gave you wings and its valleys were full of wonderful flowers. I have a long-acquired habit of associating a certain phrase in the Lord's Prayer with the most beautiful thing I have seen during the day, and if I have seen nothing beautiful, and have been leading a dull life in a town, my mind goes roving back to certain wondrous sights in the past. Most frequently of all it goes to the wastes, covered with crimson poppies, in Russian Central Asia, and occasionally to the verdure and splendour of the Altai and the delphiniums there, the blue, purple and yellow monkshood, the China-blue larkspurs, blue and purple larkspurs. A wonderful place for flowers. Here are sweeps of blue sage, mauve cranesbills poking everywhere, saffron poppies, grass of Parnassus, campanula, pink moss flowers and giant thistle-heads, gentian, Siberian iris.

Just outside the Cossack settlement it was late summer, and the glossy peony fruits were turning crimson from green, opening to show rows of black teeth—seeds. But as you climbed upward toward the snow the season changed, and it was possible to recover the lost spring.

The southern side of the mountains seemed to be very bare, but our side, the northern one, was green. It was comparatively easy to reach districts where it might be thought no foot of man had ever trod—primeval moss-grown forest, where were no tracks, no flowers, nothing but firs and moss. Numberless trees had fallen, and the moss had grown over them, and, in climbing through, one helped oneself from tree to tree, balancing and finding a footing. Above this jungle was a stretch of steep mountain-side sparsely grown with young firs, and then grey, barren, slippery rock. Wonderful shelves and chasms, fissures, precipices, and ways up without ways down, boulder-strewn tracks and founts of bubbling water, milk-white streams, crystal streams.

I was housed very well with a prosperous Cossack family, and, except for the fact that there was a terrible monotony in their dinners, had no reason to complain. Every evening when I returned there was beef "cutlets," white scones and butter, a jug of milk, and the samovar. The whole family was in the fields hay-making all day, and were indisposed to give time to cooking.

Most days I spent by the side of a little mountain river, where I built a sort of causeway out of rocks, diverted the channel, made a deep bathing-pool—enthralling occupations. Here also I had a bonfire, made coffee, baked potatoes, cooked red currant jam. Strips of red currants hung like bunting on some of

ALTAISKA *STANITSA*: VIEW OF MOUNT BIELUKHA

the bushes, and were so thick that you could pick a potful in a quarter of an hour. Here also I sorted out and re-read thirty or forty copies of *The Times*, saved up for me, with letters, at the post office of Semipalatinsk—all the details of the political quarrel over Ulster, the resignation of Sir John French (as he was then called), of Colonel Seely, the vigorous speeches of Mr. John Ward, the brilliant defences of Mr. Asquith. We seemed to be running forward silently and smoothly to an exciting rebellion or civil war in Ireland, and nobody seemed to deplore the prospect of strife. The Government, nominally in favour of peace at all costs, were incapable of preventing their opponents obtaining arms, and were, therefore, allowing their friends to arm. On the whole we seemed to be tired of the dull blessings of peace, out of patience with peace. Yet we were not ready for the strife that was coming, though certainly in a mood to take arms. It is astonishing that with our many international characters—those diplomatical journalists of ours—we did not know what was coming, or no one was at pains to undeceive us. Journalists abroad, even if they are out of touch with Courts and are uninfluential, have yet much greater opportunities for understanding international situations than Foreign Offices. Why is it that they nearly always mislead? In our country a certain glamour overspreads the personality of the polyglot who writes of foreign Courts and foreign policies, but as an observer of the Press for many years I can give it as my opinion that, as a nation, we do not gain much from the pens of those journalists who run in and out of chancelleries and are well known at foreign Courts. In any case, as regards those who dealt specially with Germany, Austria and the Balkans at the time of the outbreak of war, they were either blind or ignorant, which is unthinkable, or mixed up somehow in the great German intrigue.

Silence reigned in Europe, and under cover of that silence what tremendous preparations were being made, what hurrying to and fro there was. It is astonishing to look back now to those serene and happy weeks in the Altai and to feel the contrast of the innocence of Nature and the devilish conspiracy in the minds of men. If there are devils in the world, black spirits as opposed to white spirits, what triumph was theirs, what hidden ecstasy as at the coming triumph of negation. Behind the screen of this silence horns were blowing announcing the great feasts of death, the blasting of the temples wherein the spirit of man dwells, the orgy of ugliness and madness. But being, happily, untuned to this occult world, we did not hear them.

It was holiday time, the end of July, the Englishman's great liberation moment when, even if he goes on working in office or factory, he ceases to work hard and lazes at his work. His wife and family have gone to the seaside. He will join them in a week or so. Meanwhile he is "camping out at home." The young man is buying stout boots and greasing them for tramping, is scanning maps and guidebooks, and making absurd tables of mileage, prospec-

MOBILISATION DAY ON THE ALTAI: THE VILLAGE EMPTIED OF ITS FOLK

tive hotel bills and expenses. The teachers, with the children, are liberated from the schools, and the former are gone on Polytechnic tours and what not, whilst the latter chalk mysterious diagrams on the pavement and play hop-scotch, or play "Wall-flowers, wallflowers, growing up so high," or "This is the way she went." The unfashionable but numerous marriages take place of those who must make the honeymoon coincide with annual leave, and the happy couples take Cook's tickets to Strasburg, to the Tyrol, to Munich.

And those Russians who *must* escape their fellow-Russians, and don't like the bad drains of their own watering-places, are off to German baths and Bohemian and Austrian spas. Students are tripping across to Switzerland. And on all in German territory the guillotine of war is going to fall. At all the money-changers' offices at Charing Cross and in the City you can buy German marks, though there is not much gold to be had. French gold, English, Russian can be had in almost any quantities, and Cook's will sell you German hotel tickets for all August.

One lazy July afternoon I sat on the wooden steps leading up to my veranda and talked with a Cossack on wars in general, what prospects of war there actually were at that moment; and we concluded that there might possibly be war with Austria. It was the idlest talk, but the Cossack lives for a new war, and I did not like to discourage him. He for his part rather hoped for a nearer war; one with China would suit him, but he'd thankfully consider a war with Austria if nothing else were available.

I went along the exterior street of the village to the little post office facing the wall of the White Ones, as they call the Altai, and talked with the postmaster about marals, and he closed the office to go out and show me where his garden was. Here also were several *maralniki*, and I found them when clambering up the ridges, and the deer, seeing me, would scamper away. The village had a butter factory, and I used to go there and wait during the last stages of production for a pound of butter, and, sitting on a bucket upside down, chatted with other villagers. Opposite the cottage where I stayed lived the priest, and he often came across and talked. The church was the next building after the priest's house, and was a beautiful little wooden temple built by the peasants themselves. I was quickly in the midst of the life of the settlement, and when the news came I was at once thought to be the obvious person to apply to for information. On the 30th of July, after a long day on the mountains, I slept serenely on the overcoats on the floor of my Cossack habitation. Next morning came the young horseman with the red flag flying from his shoulder, and the tremendous excitement and clamour of the reception of the *ukase* to mobilise for war. As I wrote when I described this in "Russia and the World," the Cossacks were not told with whom the war was or would be, and one of the first surmises that they made was that the war must be with England—crafty old England, who always stood in Russia's way and was siding with the Turks again. Or she was afraid Russia was going to attack India.

The real news came at last, and with it the necessity to return to Europe as soon as possible. The war came across my summer as it came across the summer of thousands of others, cutting life into two very distinct parts. At the village of Altaisky I must draw my war line dividing past and present, one part of life from this other new astonishing part. The story of my journey has drawn to its close. Before, however, leaving the subject of Russian Central Asia I would give the thoughts and reflections that the journey has suggested, and especially those referring to Anglo-Russian rivalry in empire, the questions of India and Constantinople, the future of our friendship and of the two empires.

APPENDIX I

RUSSIA AND INDIA AND THE PROSPECTS OF ANGLO-RUSSIAN FRIENDSHIP

THE prospects of Anglo-Russian friendship are very fair at the moment of writing, the after-the-war prospects. Generally speaking, international amity or hostility has heretofore depended on the absence or presence of clashing interests. Russia does not stand on our road of Empire, and has never fought us and could never fight us commercially as Germany has done. Our only doubt about Russia has been as to her possible designs on India. Fifty years ago there were few Englishmen who did not entertain expectations of eventual war with Russia, and after the annexation of Merv, and the running of the Central Asian Railway thither, Beaconsfield was obliged to assure us that the keys of India were to be found in London, and consisted in the spirit and determination of the British people. We felt we were secure because we could fight Russia and did not fear her. As Lord Curzon wrote in his book on Russian Central Asia:

"The day that a Russian army starts forth from Balkh for the passes of the Hindu Kush, or marches out of the southern gate of Herat *en route* for

Kandahar, we may say, as Cromwell did at Dunbar: 'Now hath the Lord delivered them into my hand.'"

Our other bond of security lay in the fact that the Russians knew they could not successfully attack us. Though it must be said now, after our thwarted efforts against the Turks on Gallipoli and our experience in Mesopotamia, that it is not clear that we could count on winning a distant war of invasion. Though we are increasing daily in military power and sagacity, as a result of fighting the Germans, we are not so military a nation as we were in the days of the Crimean War. But the invasion of India by Russia may well be put out of the head once and for all. No statesman in Russia ever seriously contemplated it, and in this country those statesmen who thought of it either decried the idea or used it as a political bogey. As Namirovitch Danchenko said recently: "From my seventy years' knowledge of Russian life, I should say that the people who dreamt about the conquest of India could be found in Russia only in a madhouse." No serious steps were ever taken to thwart Russian imperial policy in Central Asia, and all that fear has brought about was mistrust and a refusal to enter into partnership with Russia in certain schemes in Asia.

The Russians have been ready to trust us for a long time, and they were anxious for an Anglo-Russian agreement even at the time when the invasion of India bogey was most in the air here.

Probably the Germans, those persistent enemics of Anglo-Russian friendship, were responsible for a great deal of subterranean propaganda in England. Many in England were pro-Russian—Gladstone (though, of course, even Gladstone asked for a war credit on one occasion of fear of Russia), Carlyle, Froude, Kinglake—there was a real basis of sympathy. But the poisoners of the mind of the British people succeeded. What an interesting glimpse of popular feeling is found in Burnaby's "Ride to Khiva" if we read it now. There is a certain poignancy in his remarks. Consider this passage to-day:

"Another peculiarity in several Russians which I remarked . . . was their desire to impress upon my mind the great advantage it would be for England to have a civilised neighbour like Russia on her Indian frontier; and when I did not take the trouble to dissent from their views—for it is a waste of breath to argue with Russians about this question—how eager they were for me to impress their line of thought upon the circle of people with whom I was most immediately connected. Of course, the arguments brought forward were based upon purely philanthropic motives, upon Christianity and civilisation. They said that the two great Powers ought to go together hand in glove; that there ought to be railways all through Asia, formed by Anglo-Russian companies; that Russia and England had every sympathy in common which should unite them; that they both hated Germany and loved France; that

England and Russia could conquer the world, and so on.

"It was a line of reasoning delightfully Russian, and though I was not so rude as to differ from my would-be persuaders, and lent an attentive ear to all their eloquence, I could not help thinking that the mutual sympathy between England and Germany is much greater than that between England and Russia; that the Christian faith as practised by the lower orders in Russia is pure paganism in comparison with the Protestant religion which exists in Prussia and Great Britain; that Germany and Great Britain are natural allies against Russia . . . that Germans and Englishmen understand by the term 'Russian civilisation' something diametrically opposite to what is attributed to it by those people who form their ideas of Muscovite progress from the few Russians they meet abroad."

Burnaby's remarks seem pretty foolish in 1916. And his views are representative of the views of many English in 1875. Prussia, whom he admires so, had just crushed the French whilst we stood by. The Boer War had not come. The Kaiser had not sent his telegram to Kruger. Our military conceit had not been taken out of us; and so, when Russia offers Britannia the hand of friendship, Britannia round her draws her cloak and folds her arms.

But Russia was sincere. She admired the English. She alone of Continental nations appreciated the spirit of Dickens and our Victorian novelists. England was still the foolish friend of Turkey, it is true, but she was not *perfide Albion.* Nor was she simply "Mr. Cotton," as Ibsen dismissed us, or "a nation of shopkeepers." From the first Russia has had some sort of *flair* for the English gentleman, has seen the best thing in our race; and their wish for friendship with us has been a sentimental matter, not a desire for commercial partnership, not a bond of sympathy between revolutionary Russia and our Socialists. The desire for friendship with England dates to before the emergence of our Socialists as a party in England. It is a genuine craving for mutual understanding between the real Russia and the real England.

Fortunately, that desire on Russia's part found an answer on this side. We became friends—we are now brothers-in-arms against a common foe. If the shedding of blood for a common ideal strengthens friendship, we should be good friends for this generation at least. Those who are young now will keep in remembrance the stress of these days, the sacrifice, the common sadness, the shared triumph. Holy Russia has become near to us, and, despite all machinations and insinuations, will remain near. And, with the hope of making things more easy, let me indicate the points of resistance to Russian friendship still remaining in our national life.

I. *India.*—A number of our people, chiefly on the Unionist side in politics, still fear Russian designs on India, and for that reason deny Russia the right to Constantinople and the Straits, should she take them. In doing this they unwittingly play the German game, which is to reserve Constantinople for Germany. There are several European journalists in the pay of Germany, and among other things they do for their money is the stirring up of British suspicion about Constantinople and Russia. The fact is that this is Russia's legitimate outlet, her front door, and there can be no settled peace in Europe as long as it is barred up or liable to be barred. It is also the seat and capital of the Russian faith, and what in 1876 Dostoieffsky answered to the question on what high ground Russia demanded Constantinople from Europe is still true:

"As the leader of Orthodoxy, as protectress and prescrver of Orthodoxy, the rôle predestined for Russia since the days of Ivan III. . . . that the nations professing Orthodoxy may be unified under her, that the Slav nations may know that her protection is the guarantee of their individual personality and the safeguard against mutual hostility. Such a union would not be for the purpose of political aggression and tyranny, not a matter of commercial gain. No, it will be a raising of Christ's truth, preserved in the East, a real new raising of Christ's Cross, and the conclusive word of Orthodoxy at the head of which will be Russia. . . . And if anyone holds that the 'new word' which Russia will speak is 'utopia,' worthy only of mockery, then I must be numbered among the Utopians——"

Still, it must be said that at the present moment Constantinople does not seem likely to fall as a fruit to the Allies or to Russia, and unless Bulgaria should turn upon her unnatural allies there is not much question of St. Sophia becoming Christian again. We ought only to keep in mind that Russia has striven for Constantinople not to have a base from which to oppose us, but in order to keep the door of her own house and to be Queen of the Eastern Church.

The next point, and where the question of India causes us to be suspicious, is that of Persia. Here, happily, some understanding has been obtained and spheres of influence allotted; but our distrust has stood in the way of the consummation of one of the most interesting schemes of the century: the trans-Persian railway. If this railway had been built before the outbreak of this world war, it would have been of extraordinary value to the Allies, an effectual means of checking the inflammation of Islam. There will be little money left when the war is over, but certainly the overland route to India should be one of the first big civilising schemes to receive attention. World railways, instead of little bits of lines, belong to the future of the Old World, and we can have them now or put it off for another era. It depends on the faith and imagination of our generation. Then Persia falls inevitably under European surveillance, and there is no reason for English and Russians at the outposts of Empire to compete and be jealous and suspicious and to squabble.

For the rest, Russian Central Asia raises no further problems. It is a peaceful, growing Russian colony, shut away from the chances of attack by foreign Powers—likely to remain for a thousand years one of the most peaceful places upon earth. Unlike India, it is comparatively empty and its peoples are decaying. The railways which Russia has built were built in order to subdue the Tekintsi and the Afghans. The railways which she is building have in view only the convenience of the colonists, the development of the colony, and trade with China. Russia is slow out there, and she is laying the sound foundations of a healthy and happy colonial country.

II. *Rivalry of Empire.*—Whatever be the direct issue of the war with Germany, one indirect result seems certain: England will have more empire, whilst Germany will have less, and Russia will not lose anything. Two great empires will emerge more clearly, facing one another because of the dispersal of the German ambition. There seems to be only one possibility of German extension, and that lies in the chance of Germans and Austrians turning on their own allies and absorbing Bulgaria and Turkey. But that chance must be considered remote to-day. The Russian and the British Empires will stand facing one another in friendly comparison. The Russian Empire is self-supporting, it has no need to import the necessities of life—food, fuel, raiment; whereas we could support ourselves, but do not, not having reconciled our self-hostile commercial interests. For many a long day Russia will export for British consumption corn, butter, eggs, sugar, wool, and wood, to say nothing of other things. And when at last we succeed in making our own Empire independent, the Russians will eat their butter themselves and there will be more white bread on the peasant's table. It will be no calamity for Russia.

I was speaking on the future of the Russian Empire at one of our leading Conservative clubs in London last winter, and I was surprised to note a very important feeling of opposition toward Russia. Those who were interested in manufactures wanted the tariff against British goods reduced, and those who were Imperialist in spirit felt a certain jealousy and suspicion of the Russian Empire. Several speakers warned Russia that she had better give up the dream of having Constantinople—it would be bad for her health if she were to have it. But the most significant utterance came from an ardent tariff reformer, who did not know how far love of Russia was compatible with love of the British Empire, for more Russian grain coming to us meant less Canadian grain, and so on. If we gave Russia any preferential treatment as regards her exports to us, we handicapped our own colonies. We ought to give our colonies preferential terms, but how would the Russians feel if we asked for reduced tariffs for the import of our manufactured goods into Russia while at the same time we put a tax on the produce they sent to us. That problem is a serious one, and it cannot be doubted that the best policy for us is to make ourselves self-dependent as an Empire whatever it may cost us in foreign favour. Russia must not misunderstand our efforts to consolidate the Empire, and I do not think she will. The diminution in our import of food-stuffs from Russia will be gradual, and will be made up partially by the increased import of other things which Russia has in superabundance. Yet even as regards ores and mineral products we have to learn to be self-supporting. The war itself, which shuts us off from Russia and throws us upon our own resources, has sent us to our own colonies. We are beginning to find in the Empire not only our food, but also the raw materials required for our products. Take, for instance, the case of asbestos. The only first-class quality of asbestos in the world comes from the Urals, and it is a product of great value industrially. During the war it has been very difficult to get it from Russia. The result has been that we have found a very good though still inferior quality in Rhodesia, and may quite conceivably obtain all our best supplies from that colony in time, the lower grades coming from Canada, which begins to have a great output. But our tendency to be self-dependent will tend to rid Russia of many exploiting foreign companies, and for that the Russian people will be thankful. They want to experience what gifts they have for doing things for themselves.

III. *The Trade Treaty.*—Russia will be so much in debt to us financially at the end of the war that there will be a tendency to regard her as an insolvent liability company possessing valuable assets. Some of our business men may want to treat her as such and appoint a trustee, so to say. There is a movement to inflict upon Russia a trade treaty similar to that, or even more humiliating than that which Germany called upon her to sign. The bond of friendship with Russia cannot be a commercial halter round her neck. She would quickly resent foreign financial control, no matter from what quarter it might be exercised. Russia will be all but bankrupt after the war, and all that she will have lost will have been lost for the common cause. We should be generous to her and see what can be done, not to tie her and bind her industrially and financially, but for us all. Russia herself is ready to make a kindly treaty providing us with real advantages over Germany, but she could not make a treaty whereby arrangements would be made for the paying off of her financial war debts to her allies.

IV. *The Basis of Friendship.*—The basis of friendship with Russia is not really trade, and no provision needs to be made to make a trade basis. We had plenty of trade with Germany or Germany with us, and that did not make for friendship. On the contrary, the question of trade and of haggling over money is almost certain in the long run to lead to estrangement, or, at least, mutual dis-esteem. There has been a growing trade, but that has not led to the growing friendship. Friendship has been founded on real mutual admiration. We like the Russians, and they like us. The positive side of Russia profoundly interests us. Of course, we are not vitally interested in the negative side, the rotten conditions of life in certain classes, the faults of Russia, the seamy side of the picture. We are thoroughly aware of the ugliness of the negative side of our own life, and we would ask—do not judge us by that, that is not England. Similarly, in Russia we are interested in beautiful and wonderful Russia, in Holy Russia, not in unholy Russia. This positive side is comparatively unrealised here, for gossip and slander make more noise than truth, but in it is a great treasure both for Russia and for ourselves in friendship. On the whole the prospects are good.

APPENDIX II

THE RUSSIAN EMPIRE AND THE BRITISH EMPIRE

THE moment of peace will be the moment of reconsideration. We shall want to know where we all stand, and we shall want to face the facts—financially, individually, imperially. We shall want to know what we have got, what we owe, what sort of empire we have to make or mar in the succeeding years, what are its resources, what its possibilities, and ours. One may remark, in passing, what very good work is being done by the Confederation of the Round Table.* The calculation is exercising many patriotic British minds. First of all be it remarked, in order to remove misconceptions, we British people are not by any means the most numerous white people. We have in our Empire something like 63 million whites, whereas Russia has at least 140 million, Germany has 65 million, and the United States have 82 million of mixed race. We compare favourably with the United States because we are homogeneous and much more calm in soul, and favourably with Germany because she has no land for expansion, though it must be remembered that if Austria and Germany should unite, the Germans would have almost as large a white population as

* See "The Round Table," a review of the interests of the Empire, and "The Prospect of a Commonwealth," an extraordinary after-the-war volume.

Russia, and certainly a very much more active one. There remains Russia, with its enormous population and its astonishingly extensive territory. Russia has ample room for ten times her present population, and she has it at her back door, as it were. She has no oceans to cross. The railway goes all the way or can go all the way from Petrograd to the uttermost ends of her earth. She has also calm, and can develop without worry. As an empire, compared with ours, she has tremendous advantages. Her people are not impatient to be rich, the strain of her race is not confused through foreign immigration, she is shut off from mongrelising influences, and tends to grow with pure blood and a clear understanding of her own past and her own destiny. She has less chance of making mistakes. And, as I have said, her problems are much simpler. It is not difficult to keep the stream of colonisation moving into the emptiness of Asia when the railways are so good as to carry one six thousand miles for thirteen roubles, a little over a sovereign.

Our younger politicians have got to decide what they are working for—trade, or the Empire, or the people, or the individual. They must affirm a larger policy than has been affirmed heretofore, a world policy, and they must not scorn the lessons which Germany has taught them: the necessity to be thorough, to have large conceptions, and to work for the realisation of these large conceptions rather than potter about doctoring the little-English constitution here and giving a little funeral there. We teach our children a very foolish little proverb: that if we look after the pence the pounds will look after themselves. That is the opposite of the truth, which is, that if we look after the pounds we need never worry our heads about the pennies. If we nationalised our ocean-transit, we should not need to insure our working men against unemployment. If we scheduled the enormous tracts of land available for culture in the Empire, we should not need to wage war with the landowners in Great Britain.

Our present Colonial Minister, Mr. Bonar Law, has risen to the front as the political leader of our Conservative and Imperialist party. He does not seem to love party strife, and he has, perhaps, found a permanent post at the Colonial Office. He is the next man of importance after Mr. Joseph Chamberlain, and though by no means so great a man, he is an admiring follower of the great Imperialist. Whatever we may think of the merits of Free Trade and Protection, Chamberlain was undoubtedly right in his larger conception of a unified British Empire, a *Zollverein*. And the Liberals who opposed him and confused the issue were merely opportunists. They were not concerned to find what they could agree with in his proposals. They merely fought him to beat him and step into his shoes politically. The riff-raff of political opportunists set on him, and he was forced to shed one of his great illusions, a trust in the common sense of the people. Mr. Bonar Law is his successor, and we wish him well. He might well carry his office out of the arena of party politics and sit at the Colonial Office whatever wind were blowing. For Imperial Policy must have continuity if it is to be successful.

England must hope and pray that Mr. Law has given up mere politics. We are thoroughly sick of the bad-tempered quarrelling and malicious fighting of the heads of the parties. Even a first-rate man is ninth-rate when he is quarrelling, and a quarrel among politicians is always a quarrel among ninth-rate politicians. Political genius likes affirmation and agreement. The task of Mr. Bonar Law is to think about the Empire and gain consciousness of its true destiny; it is not to think out devices in political antagonism. As a nation we demand he give his whole time and the cream of his intellect to the positive task of giving to every citizen of the Empire the consciousness of the large thing. He will be attacked; curs will bark at him; the Germans and German Jews will try and stir up the uneducated against him; there will be all manner of insinuations. But he need never reply or attempt to defend himself. The nation and the Empire will back him calmly. There is a splendid Russian tale of a prince climbing a mountain to obtain a bird, and all the stones behind him shout abuse after him. He is safe on his quest on this condition only, that he does not turn round and listen, or draw his sword to attack. If he turn he will change to a stone himself. The point is, we are going to be more in need of great men once this war is over than we ever were before—of great men with big ideas, faith that they can be realised, and that calm of spirit which is the greatest strength.

If Mr. Bonar Law is not great enough, or if he'd rather continue in the political arena, there is another man for the post, and that is Lord Milner. Lord Milner strikes one as the greater man. The Empire is his one idea. He thinks largely—his imagination takes him in vast sweeps over the surface of the Empire. He has dignity, is a powerful speaker, and a clear thinker on Imperial matters. His weakness is a certain aloofness or reserve, an ambassadorial manner, and one is not quite sure what is behind it. Mr. Bonar Law, on the other hand, is unscreened; he is familiar, even domestic in his manner. Probably what Mr. Law has to guard against is doing things in small parcels, doing branch things rather than root things, whereas Lord Milner may give offence occasionally by a lack of consideration for other people's feelings—want of tact, in fact. In any case they are both men on whom the eyes of the nation rest. Lord Milner has sent me an extremely interesting letter which had been addressed to him by a number of British citizens who have become lost to the British Empire. By his kind permission I reproduce it:

"*Open Letter to Lord Milner.*

"QUINCY, MASS., U.S.A.

"*Dec. 15th*, 1915.

"LORD MILNER,—I have read with intense interest the report of your speech appearing in *The Times*

Weekly Edition of Nov. 19th. You mentioned the indifference of the working man to Imperial affairs. I am a working man, and possibly my views on these questions may be of some small interest to you. When I speak of my views I mean that they also are the views of other workers with whom I come in contact. I mix daily with several dozen workers, British born, and I assure you that the opinions here expressed are the opinions of practically all.

"We believe that right now a strong committee should be formed to deal with Imperial reconstruction after the war. This committee should have a well thought out, clearly defined, and decisive policy to put in operation the moment the war ends. We believe that not less than half a million soldiers who have fought in the war should be settled in Canada, Australasia and U.S. Africa, and that an appropriation of not less than one billion* pounds sterling should be voted for the purpose. Canada is a land of vast agricultural possibilities and great mineral wealth. A small group of the best agricultural and engineering experts in the Empire should be sent over to make all necessary preparations for the coming of the men. The exact location or locations where they are to settle should be defined, lines of branch railways should be surveyed, sites of model garden cities, cement built, should be located, mining properties surveyed, and the location of factories and workshops should be decided upon. Nothing should be left to chance. The gang ploughs, threshing

* American value, i.e. £1,000,000,000.

machines, motor tractors, grain elevators, etc., should be provided and run on the co-operative principle, and the entire properties should belong to the nation. If one-half the energy, foresight, and preparation used in the war were used for the reconstruction, the scheme is an assured success.

"There are great irrigation and artesian possibilities in S. Africa. Preparations should be made *now*. Incidentally the intensely loyalist stock thus settled would swamp the Hertzog party with their disruptive ideals. In Australia very great possibilities await irrigation. I have only to point out what has been done in arid S. California and Arizona to prove this.

"The British Empire heretofore has been more or less imaginary; there has been nothing tangible about it. Take my own case, for instance. I cite it merely because it illustrates a principle. Seven years ago I was in Scotland and unemployed. There were a great many unemployed at the time. Those who had no means were left to starve. Was anything done for them? Absolutely nothing! All were British, loved Britain, were able and willing to work, yet no organisation was created to utilise their services. Personally I came to the United States. I have done better here than at home; had better pay, shorter hours, better conditions. What is the British Empire to us? Absolutely nothing; a mere sentiment. Yet our feelings are British still, our sympathies are British; but that is not enough. There must be something tangible to go on, something *real;* sentiment alone is no use. An Englishman here whom

I meet daily is a veteran of the S. African war. When that war finished he was not allowed to settle in S. Africa. At home he could not get work. He was driven to want. He had to pawn his medal to live, and finally was assisted to America. He has done well here and has been steadily employed. But he has been embittered, and his sentiment in his own words is: 'To hell with the British Empire.' It is an empty phrase to him, without meaning; and I tell you, with all the earnestness of which I am capable, that these things will mean the decline and fall of the Empire if they do not stop. In the United States there are several million British born who are lost to the Empire for ever. Their sentiments are British, their sympathies are British, but their interests are here, and interest becomes sentiment. And observe that their children born here have *sentiment* as well as interest for the land of their birth.

"The British Empire is the largest in the world. In natural resources it is the wealthiest. It could support a population of hundreds of millions in a high degree of prosperity. The British are an able and intelligent people. The nation is rich. The problem is to settle the people throughout the Empire and develop its resources under the guidance of experts, according to a well thought out and definite plan. This plan wants to take shape now. If the war were to suddenly end one year hence, and an army of three million men disbanded, we would (and will) be faced by industrial chaos. The problem must be placed in the hands of experts, and be so clearly worked out that when peace is declared the soldiers will be drafted without fuss to the various parts of the Empire, and immediately tackle the problems of city and railway building, agriculture and irrigation, mining and manufacturing. And these properties must be owned by the nation. These measures will create a *real* Empire in which every citizen will have a tangible interest. Each part will legislate on its own domestic affairs, and the Imperial Parliament, dealing with Imperial affairs and representative of all the Dominions, will be held in London. With such conditions you will find a strong sentiment for Free Trade within the Empire and Protection without, and also a strong desire for that universal military training which will defend what in very truth is one's own. Start this programme at once, and do it thoroughly, and you can be absolutely certain of a solid and enthusiastic backing.—Believe me, yours sincerely, "WM. C. ANDERSON."

Under Mr. Anderson's signature appeared the signatures of forty-nine men, all British subjects once, people of pure race and complete British traditions, now "lost to the Empire." The letter was endorsed thus:

J. C. COLLINGWOOD, late of Glasgow, Scotland;
A. W. COATES, late of York, England;
JAMES J. BYRNES, late of Dublin, Ireland;
T. GIBBONS, late of Newfoundland;

and so on, a list far too long to quote here but most impressive in its implication—"late of Great

Britain, now and henceforth of the United States of America."

I will add a letter sent to me from Tasmania, for it will help to give the atmosphere of the problem:

"9 GARDEN CRESCENT,
"HOBART, TASMANIA,
"AUSTRALIA.
"*Oct. 3rd,* 1915.

"DEAR SIR,—I am just being interested in your book, 'Russia and the World.' I read it because I was delighted with your vagabond trip along the Euxine shores. You deal with the problems of the British Empire. Perhaps you might like to get a view from 'down under'? Well, I do not consider in the matter of defence that a huge land empire has advantages over a sea empire. Russia is to-day more vulnerable than the British Empire. Let us suppose the British Isles with a navy such as it possesses to-day, with a million men ready for home defence, and with an expeditionary force of 250,000 men—'ready' at an hour's notice to step into transports also ready. Let us assume that two years' provision of corn is stored, and a tunnel with France. Let us also assume that every available rood of British ground is cultivated. What country could invade and conquer the British Isles? What country could keep up a two-years' naval war? Let us come to Australia—grand in her isolation. We shall soon have a quarter of a million of trained soldiers. We launched a new cruiser last week, and we are going to build submarines. We can not only defend ourselves, but we could supply garrisons for India. So far as external aggression is concerned, South Africa is safe. Canada is liable to attack from the Americans, and in the course of time will be attacked. If the British expeditionary army were landed promptly, and Canada had our plan of compulsory service, the Empire would be right there. India is safe except from Russia.

"Have we a weak spot as an Empire? Certainly we have. England for three parts of a century has allowed herself to be bled to death by the emigration of her best youth to foreign countries. That ought to be stopped. There should be an export tax of £20 upon every emigrant to the United States or other alien country. (Plain talk about U.S.A.) As to the present 'colonies'—hateful title—there are but two British ones within the Empire—Australia and New Zealand. The others have an undesirable mixture of races. It should be a portion of the Imperial policy to fill up Canada and South Africa with British-born people. But such emigration must be upon a system. Under a proper system we could do with two millions of immigrants in Australia. Suddenly dumped upon our wharves, 1,000 would be an inconvenience. Your scheme of cheap ships is admirable. When we build railways in Australia, and provide water schemes, we do not consider whether they will 'pay,' but whether they will develop the country and add to the happiness of the people. The best method of emigration is to dispatch from the United Kingdom every year, say, 500,000 youths and girls from 15 years of age and upwards. These would find homes *at low wages* in settlers' families in Canada, South Africa and Australia, and would become acclimatised and absorbed into the population. This emigration should be a State scheme and COMPULSORY. But the emigrants should not be made slaves of. When their indentures ended they should be allowed, if they wished, to return to England in one of your ships free of charge. I do not wish to enlarge upon the subject, but the failures of adult English immigrants who come here are pathetic. They cannot get along, neither would we get along in England. The immigrant should be captured young. This is the greatest problem of the Empire:

"(1) To fill up the Empire with loyal citizens of pure British birth.

"(2) In the cases of Canada and South Africa, to send large numbers in order to neutralise the alien elements now existing there. To stop foreign immigration into British territories, especially German immigration.

"Upon the question of naturalisation we have been too easy and indifferent. A man wishing to be naturalised should make a solemn application in *propria persona* before a court. He should be under the obligation to abjure his foreign nationality and to take a British name. We have now our directories crowded with foreign names, which through generations of intermarriages have lost their original national significance.

"I note that you compare our culture with that of America. Thanks! No two countries could be more dissimilar—there is not amongst us the greed, the wild rush, or the boastfulness of the Americans. We do not like them. While we are on comparisons, let me remind you that while you have failed to adjust your Irish question, we have federated Australia, a task of no small difficulty. While you have been talking and spilling ink about conscription, we have a system of compulsory training, both for the army and the navy, in full operation. While you allow strikes in the midst of war, our difficulties are being settled by wages boards and arbitration courts. We are not perfect, but our Press is much superior in tone and culture to yours. It is painful to read some of your Yankeeised London papers. In literature we have given you Mrs. Humphry Ward, though to learn new sins we read the indecent novels which appear to be the chief product of British fiction. And we have given the world—Melba!

"As to our share of the war. I walked down-street in Hobart yesterday to take a 'billy'—pity your simplicity if you do not know what that is—to the City Hall. It was filled with all sorts of good things for our boys at Gallipoli for Christmas. Outside the newspaper office I read the cable, another ghastly list of Australian casualties. Were they necessary? Could not the Turks have been outflanked and their communications cut? When I reached home my wife and her friend were knitting socks for the soldiers. The lady friend mentioned, be it correct or not, that a ship that declined to carry troops—the *Wimmera*, New Zealand to Melbourne—was taken possession of and forced to take the men. The streets are full of soldiers ready to sail, and, alas, with many returned from the war crippled for life. And such splendid young men. What an improved edition of the British race the Australians are!

"Enough from stranger to stranger, but as your book seems to indicate gleams of intelligence on your part, and as it interested me, I am humbly—as a native-born Australian now close approaching the Psalmist's limit—endeavouring to repay the compliment.—Yours truly, "WILLIAM CROOKE."

And Mr. Crooke enclosed a poem on the launching of H.M.S. *Brisbane* at the naval dockyard at Cockatoo Island:

Another link in the steel-strong chain which holds us heart to heart,
Another pledge to the old, old vow which swears we'll never part;
While life doth last and love doth last we'll give thee of our own—
Dear Motherland, accept this gift we lay before thy throne.

Forged in the heat of a southern sun, framed 'neath an Austral sky,
Worthy indeed this ship shall be to float thy flag on high.
Fanned by the breath of a South Sea breeze, kissed by the foam-flecked spray,
Did ever a child of War awake as this one wakes to-day?

We bargain not in windy words, and not in idle boast,
We speed her sliding down the slip, and make her name a toast.
Remember ye that gaunt, grey wreck on Cocos' barren rocks [*Emden*],
Where seagulls pick the whitened bones around the old sea-fox.

Another link in the steel-strong chain which holds us heart to heart,
Another hound slipped from the leash to play a winning part;
Her flag is broken to the wind, her steel has met the sea—
Dear Motherland, accept the gift we give this day to thee.

The letters indicate something of the spirit of our people, and they more than touch on the "after-the-war" problems of the Empire. Both indicate the way we lose our citizens to the United States of America. And it is, of course, loss to the Empire whenever an Englishman settles in the U.S.A. Our social interchange with the United States is a snare for us. The gleam of their dollars is the Star-spangled Banner, and not the Union Jack. We do not see that, although the Americans speak a recognisable dialect of our language, they are a foreign people, with their own national interests. When a man or woman goes there to settle he is lost to us, and if in the great unrest after the war a great number of our young people set sail for "God's own country," it will mean that we can add the numbers of those young people to the total of our casualties. That is clear.

Then we cannot afford to imitate the ways of the U.S.A. The U.S.A. receive the discontented and rebellious of all nations in Europe—it is Europe's safety-valve. Our Irish go there, German anti-militarists, Russian Jews and Finns, Austrian Slavs and what not. The nature of the United States is composite and its task is synthesis. The nature of our Empire is elementary and its task is to keep pure. Canada has made a mistake in opening its doors to aliens, and especially to those aliens who would stand a poor chance of passing the tests at Ellis Island. Canada behaves as if it were left behind in the struggle by America, as if she had been asleep in the past and was now making up for lost ground by any and every means. She is virtually accepting those aliens whom the U.S.A. consider not good enough to take. Through the help of Tolstoy and the Quakers the Dukhobors were dumped down on Canadian soil. They have refused to become naturalised British subjects, and have sacrificed estates to the value of over three million dollars—" in the name of the equality of all people upon earth we would not be naturalised, and we sacrificed this material fortune." They learn no English, conform to no English rules, nourish no English sentiments, are lost to Russia, and are no use to us. The same may be said of the hundreds of thousands of other aliens we are letting in. It should be obvious that to lose British-born citizens, our own spirit, flesh and blood, in the United States, and at the same time to take those aliens who cannot pass the doctor and the immigration examination at New York, is a woeful and even ridiculous circumstance.

After the war America will be extremely rich and we extremely poor. She will be in a position to buy everything that is offered for sale. We must take care not to offer birthrights in any shape or form. That which we can legitimately sell let us sell, but that which is in the nature of an heirloom of the British people let us not be tempted to sell, no matter how high the mountain of dollars be piled on the American shore or how dazzlingly it may shine in the sunshine. I say this with no malice against the American people. They are a splendid people, and they are working out their own ideals. They are carrying out their ideals of town-planning, marriage-planning, slum-raising, park-planting, wages-raising beyond anything we dream of here. When I wrote in my book on America that we British were the dying West whereas America was the truly living West, I was taken up by British critics as if I had said something very disparaging about my own people. That was a mistake. I do not desire to see my own people a Western people, such as the Americans are, but rather a nation seated between the East and the West. Some of us fondly think ourselves Western in our ideals, but the fact is the Americans have left us far behind, and we can never catch up because we do not really believe in these ideals. But we can gain immensely by seeing America *go ahead.* Let us shake hands with America; she is splendid. God speed! Go on, work out your ideals, let us see you as you wish to be. Meanwhile we will go on with our own problems and the realisation of our own ideals.

With America on the West then also with Russia on the East—shake hands! Thanks to Russia, and God be with her also. Let her realise her ideals and discover what she is; we shall learn from the spectacle of her self-realisation. And meanwhile we will go on with our own problems and the realisation of our own ideals.

We who write about foreign countries are the torch-bearers to foreign progress and the means of foreign friendship. We render good service, and if our light shine well and show clear pictures it is unfair to reproach us with a wish to Russianise or Americanise or whatever it is. Our function is a legitimate one, and, far from confusing or alienating our readers, our hearts are actually with our own nation and we help our fellow-countrymen to see themselves as quite distinctive. Our minds certainly are confused by the writings and sayings of those stay-at-home folk who imagine that difference of nationality is only difference of speech and customs, and perhaps of dress, not understanding that first of all it is difference of soul and difference in destiny.

To return to the comparison of the two Empires and the consideration of the colonial letters, Mr. Anderson asks for an Imperial Commission to consider the "after-the-war" problems, and in conversation with Mr. Bonar Law I learn that such a Commission is to sit, and there is the possibility of an

Imperial Parliament being formed. This ought to be taken up warmly by our people at home. I also discussed with Mr. Law the prospects of emigration after the war. There is a great unrest in the Army. Great numbers of men have one common opinion that they are not going to return to the old dull grind in factory and office after the war is over. They are going in for an open-air life, going to Canada, going to Australia, or going to take up land at home in Great Britain. The Canadians and Australians have served their homelands well by telling the men at home what it is like in the far parts of the Empire. Our men have a genuine admiration for the physique of our Colonials. The fine bodies and good spirits of these men speak for themselves, and then they are full of talk of a rich country, beautiful Nature, wildness, big chances, prosperity. It is no wonder that the Englishman wants to go there also when the war is over. There will be a great readiness to go. The question is what facilities will be given them to go? How much will it cost and how much land will they be given, and what status will they have within the Empire? Mr. Law was not inclined to give much answer to that, and he reminded me that we wanted to get some more men back to the land in our own country. The back-to-the-land movement here is, however, of little importance if we are going to look upon the whole Empire as a British unity and feel that a man on the land in Australia can be of more significance than a man on the land in Essex.

I asked Mr. Bonar Law whether he thought that

our manufacturers here would be dismayed at the prospect of so many young men going to the Colonies, would they not oppose facilities being given? Would they not feel that it was necessary to keep the labour market overflowing with labour in order to keep labour cheap? In any case, would they not feel they needed to keep the men in England? The foundation of personal wealth is a plenitude of labour. The more hands employed, the richer the man at the top. Mr. Law did not think they were likely to raise objections.

The overcrowding in the United Kingdom is much greater than in France or Germany or Italy. India is also terribly overcrowded, but Canada and Australia and South Africa are practically empty. The only nation that occupies the correct amount of land proportional to its population is China. Russia has double the territory of China, and something like a third of the total population. And, thanks to cheap railway fares, the Russian population spreads quietly and naturally. After the war we must nationalise a steamship service for the use of British subjects only, and make it possible to travel anywhere in the Empire for a pound or so, paying for food according to a normal tariff. We must give emigrants privileges in our own Colonies that they would not obtain in the United States. We must set up big Imperial works, and spend time and money in development. We must not relax our rule of the seas, but go on building an ever better, ever more efficient Navy, and not underman it. We must live even more on the sea than we have done in the past, for the seas are our high roads, the connecting links of Empire. We must get out of the foolish habit of thinking of Canada and Australia and South Africa as terribly far away. It is a little world, and there is scarcely a far-away in it. We have to give to our working men, and to their children in the schools, the consciousness of belonging to a big and glorious thing rather than the consciousness of belonging to a little State that is almost played out. Let us think of Russia with her bigness, her space, her consciousness of unity, and of the large thing, and remember we have all the possibilities of health and splendour that the Russians have if we will only face our problems and do the things which are obvious to all except to those who fight in the political arena for fighting's sake.

To recapitulate:

(1) Russia has at least double the white population in her Empire that we have in ours. Why should we not take steps to transplant from overcrowded Britain to the less crowded parts of the Empire, and so get better families?

(2) The Russian Empire is all on land, and is easily strung together by railways, whereas our Empire is across seas. Fares within the Russian Empire are cheap. Why should we not popularise our ocean travel and have cheap fares on the seas?

(3) Russia, through certain natural advantages, keeps her race pure, even on the outskirts of Empire. Why should we let our own people go to the United

States, and try to fill up our Colonies with aliens who, in time of war, are ready to blow up Parliament buildings, powder factories, plot assassinations, and what not?

(4) Russia is self-supporting in food, fuel, and clothing. Why should not we be?

(5) The Duma is elected by the people not only of Russia in Europe, but by the people of the whole Russian Empire. Why should not we have Imperial representatives in the House of Commons—one man one vote for all white British citizens.

(6) The Russian Empire is a large unity with a growing consciousness of its own power. Why should not the British Empire realise similar possibilities of unity and self-expression?

Index

Index

Index

Index

Index

Index

Index

Index

Index

Index